Assembly Programming for Cyber Security

Unleash the Power of Low-Level Code to
Break and Defend Systems

Louis Madson

Discover other books in the Series

"Assembly Programming for Beginners: Master the Low Level and Control Hardware from Scratch"

"Assembly Programming for Computer Architecture: Understanding the Hardware"

"Assembly Programming for Malware Analysis: Malicious Software Development and Malware Analysis with Assembly"

"Assembly Programming for Network: Development of Communication Protocols"

"Assembly Programming for Operating Systems: Build Your Own OS from Scratch"

Disclaimer

The information provided in *"Assembly Programming for Cyber Security: Unleash the Power of Low-Level Code to Break and Defend Systems"* by Louis Madson is **for** educational and informational purposes only.

This Book is designed to introduce readers to the fundamentals of assembly programming and low-level hardware control. The author and publisher make no representations or warranties regarding the accuracy, completeness, or applicability of the content.

Introduction

In a time when digital threats are omnipresent and cyber security is critically important, it is vital to grasp the fundamental principles of computer systems. Introducing "Assembly Programming for Cyber Security: Unleash the Power of Low-Level Code to Break and Defend Systems." This book aims to provide you with the essential knowledge and skills to navigate the complex realm of assembly programming and leverage this understanding to enhance your cyber security efforts.

Assembly language acts as a conduit between high-level programming and the machine code that governs a computer's hardware. By studying assembly, you will acquire a distinctive viewpoint on how software interacts with the core architecture of computers, enabling you to identify vulnerabilities that may be hidden by high-level languages. Whether you are an emerging cyber security professional, a hacker seeking to hone your skills, or an experienced expert aiming to expand your expertise, this book presents valuable insights into the capabilities and complexities of low-level code.

Throughout the chapters, we will examine the syntax and structure of assembly language, investigate the subtleties of various architectures, and demonstrate practical applications of assembly in both offensive and defensive contexts. We will scrutinize common vulnerabilities, analyze malware, and create tools to strengthen systems against potential threats.

This journey isn't just about learning a programming language; it's about gaining critical insights into the mind of an attacker and the methodologies used to protect against them. You'll soon realize that an understanding of assembly programming opens doors to a richer understanding of system behavior—ultimately empowering you to better safeguard your networks and applications.

In the hands of a skilled practitioner, assembly language is more than a tool; it is a weapon in the ongoing war against cyber threats. As you progress through this book, you'll not only learn how to read and write in assembly but also how to think like a cyber defender who can anticipate, identify, and thwart attacks.

So, whether you're looking to break into the cyber security field, elevate your existing skills, or simply explore the exciting world of low-level programming, this book serves as your comprehensive guide to harnessing the power of assembly language. Prepare to embark on a transformative journey where the lines of code you write can become both a shield and a sword in the digital landscape. Let's get started!

Chapter 1: Introduction to Assembly for Cybersecurity

Assembly language acts as an essential intermediary between high-level programming languages and machine code. High-level languages such as Python, Java, and C++ enable developers to create code that is easily comprehensible to humans, whereas assembly language facilitates a more straightforward interaction with a computer's hardware. Each instruction in assembly language closely aligns with a specific machine code instruction tailored to a computer's architecture, making it a vital competency for professionals in cybersecurity.

In the field of cybersecurity, a comprehensive grasp of assembly language is crucial. It offers valuable insights into the interaction between software and hardware, the operation of operating systems, and the methods by which attackers exploit vulnerabilities in applications and systems. By acquiring knowledge of assembly language, security professionals can enhance their ability to analyze malware, reverse-engineer harmful software, comprehend exploits, and conduct more effective penetration testing.

1.2 The Role of Assembly Language in Cybersecurity

Assembly language plays a critical role in various aspects of cybersecurity:

Malware Analysis: To effectively analyze and mitigate malware threats, cybersecurity experts often need to disassemble binaries to understand their behavior. This process can reveal hidden functionality, such as keyloggers, data exfiltration techniques, or other malicious behaviors.

Exploitation and Penetration Testing: Cybersecurity professionals focused on offensive security need to understand how to craft and leverage exploits. Knowing how to write shellcode—a small piece of code used as the payload in the exploitation of a software vulnerability—often requires knowledge of assembly language.

Understanding Operating Systems: Most operating systems provide abstractions that simplify hardware interaction, but these abstractions can hide critical details about how systems operate. Knowledge of assembly helps cybersecurity professionals troubleshoot, analyze, and even exploit vulnerabilities present at the OS level.

Performance Optimization: Understanding assembly language can also play a vital role in performance optimization. In some cases, security tools, such as intrusion detection systems (IDS) and firewalls, require efficient processing of data to function correctly in real-time. A good grasp of assembly allows for better performance tuning of these systems.

1.3 Disassemblers and Debuggers

To work effectively with assembly language in the context of cybersecurity, practitioners often rely on tools such as disassemblers and debuggers. Disassemblers convert machine code back into assembly language, making it easier to analyze. Popular disassemblers include:

Ghidra: An open-source software reverse-engineering framework developed by the NSA.

IDAPython: A popular disassembler capable of handling multiple architectures, integrated with scripting capabilities for automation.

Radare2: An open-source tool that provides a set of utilities for reverse engineering and analyzing binaries.

Debuggers, on the other hand, allow cybersecurity professionals to step through code execution in real-time, inspect memory, and alter program execution. Tools such as GDB (GNU Debugger) and WinDbg are essential for dynamic analysis, allowing analysts to understand how a program interacts with the system and where vulnerabilities might reside.

1.4 Assembly Language Syntax and Structure

Understanding the basic syntax and structure of assembly language is paramount. While assembly language varies by architecture (such as x86, x64, ARM, etc.), certain principles are consistent:

Instructions: Each instruction typically consists of an operation code (opcode) followed by operands. For instance, `MOV AX, 1` moves the value of `1` into the AX register.

Registers: These are small storage locations in the CPU that hold data temporarily during instruction execution.

Labels and Directives: Labels help to identify specific locations in the code, while directives can provide instructions to the assembler itself, affecting how the code is assembled rather than how it executes.

1.5 Learning Assembly for Cybersecurity

As assembly language can seem daunting at first, here are some strategies for effective learning:

Start Simple: Begin with basic operations and gradually progress to more complex programming concepts. Familiarize yourself with syntax and common instructions.

Use Emulators: Tools like QEMU or Bochs can emulate processor architectures, providing a safe environment to practice assembly without needing dedicated hardware.

Practice Reverse Engineering: Use practical exercises involving disassembling and analyzing small programs. This will help solidify your understanding by applying assembly in real-world scenarios.

Engage with the Community: Participate in forums, study groups, or online classes. Resources like Capture The Flag (CTF) competitions can provide a hands-on approach to applying assembly in cybersecurity contexts.

Explore Sample Code: Analyze existing assembly code from various programs, especially focusing on exploits or vulnerability demonstrations, to gain ground-level insights into the cybersecurity implications of low-level programming.

As cyber threats continue to evolve, so does the need for cybersecurity professionals who understand the underlying principles of how software interacts with hardware.

Understanding Assembly Language

This chapter delves into the intricacies of assembly language, its significance in computer science, its relationship to hardware, and its applications in the modern programming landscape.

1.1 What is Assembly Language?

Assembly language is a low-level programming language that provides a symbolic representation of a computer's machine code. Each assembly language is specific to a particular computer architecture, meaning that the assembly language for one type of processor may be entirely different from that of another. The primary purpose of assembly language is to offer a human-readable abstraction of machine code, which consists of binary instructions understood directly by the hardware.

The key characteristics of assembly languages include:

Mnemonics: Assembly language instructions are composed of mnemonic codes that correspond to machine-level instructions. For example, the mnemonic `MOV` might be used to move data from one location to another, while `ADD` could be used to perform addition.

Labels: Assembly language allows the use of labels which serve as placeholders for memory addresses. This feature is useful in organizing code and making it easier to read and understand.

Direct Hardware Manipulation: Unlike high-level programming languages, assembly language allows programmers to interact directly with the hardware through specific instructions tailored to the architecture of the processor.

1.2 Historical Context

The roots of assembly language can be traced back to the early days of computing in the mid-20th century. As computers became more complex and their capabilities expanded, scientists and engineers needed a more efficient means of programming than writing long strings of binary code. The introduction of assembly languages was the result of this necessity, marking a pivotal transition from purely machine language to a language that was easier to comprehend and use.

Over the decades, assembly language has evolved alongside advancements in computer architecture. With the advent of microprocessors and complex instruction set computers (CISC), assembly languages also became more sophisticated, supporting a wider array of operations and features.

1.3 Why Learn Assembly Language?

While many modern programmers often favor high-level languages such as Python, Java, or C++, there are numerous reasons to appreciate and understand assembly language:

Performance Optimization: Assembly language allows for fine-tuned control over hardware, enabling optimizations that can significantly enhance performance for critical applications. This is particularly useful in systems programming, game development, and embedded systems.

Understanding of System Architecture: Learning assembly language provides insight into how computers work at a fundamental level. This knowledge is invaluable for troubleshooting, debugging, or designing hardware interfaces.

Legacy Systems: Many existing systems are built on

legacy software that relies on assembly language. Understanding it can be crucial for maintaining and upgrading these systems, particularly in industries such as telecommunications and aerospace.

Security and Reverse Engineering: A grasp of assembly is essential for fields like cybersecurity, where understanding low-level code can assist in identifying vulnerabilities and performing reverse engineering.

1.4 Basics of Assembly Language Syntax

Before jumping into more complex examples, it is crucial to grasp the basic syntax of assembly language. While the specifics can differ from one architecture to another, the following sections outline some common concepts.

1.4.1 Instruction Format

Typically, an assembly language instruction follows a specific structure:

```
<operation> <operands>
```

Operation: The mnemonic representing the instruction (e.g., `MOV`, `ADD`, `SUB`).

Operands: The targets of the operation, which can be registers, memory addresses, or immediate values.

1.4.2 Registers

Registers are small, high-speed storage locations within the CPU that hold data temporarily. Assembly language allows manipulation of these registers directly, which often leads to faster execution of programs.

1.4.3 Addressing Modes

Addressing modes determine how the operands of an instruction are accessed. Common addressing modes include:

Immediate: The operand is a constant directly specified in the instruction.

Direct: The operand's memory address is given directly.

Indirect: A register contains the address of the operand.

Indexed: Combines a base address with an offset. ## 1.5 Writing Your First Assembly Program

To solidify the concepts discussed, let's write a simple assembly program that adds two numbers and stores the result in a register. Here's an example in x86 assembly language:

```assembly
section .data
```

num1 db 5   ; First number num2 db 10   ; Second number

result db 0   ; Variable to store the result

section .text global _start

_start:

mov al, [num1] ; Load first number into AL register add al, [num2]   ; Add second number to AL register mov [result], al ; Store result in memory

; Exit program

```
mov eax, 60          ; System call for exit xor edi, edi   ;
Return code 0 syscall
```
```

In this example:

We define two bytes of data, `num1` and `num2`, and a variable `result` to store the output.

`_start` is the label marking the beginning of the program.

The program loads the first number, adds the second number, and then stores the result before exiting.

Understanding assembly language is akin to understanding the mechanics of a car; it grants insights into what happens under the hood. While it presents a steeper learning curve than high-level programming languages, the rewards are immense in terms of enhanced performance, deeper comprehension of computation, and the ability to navigate legacy systems.

## The Power of Assembly for Cybersecurity

This chapter explores the significance of assembly language in cybersecurity, its unique advantages, and how it can be wielded to fortify defenses against a landscape of ever-evolving cyber threats.

## Understanding Assembly Language

Assembly language is a low-level programming language that is closely related to a computer's machine code. Unlike high-level programming languages, which are
```

abstracted from the hardware, assembly language provides direct access to a system's architecture. This closeness enables programmers and security experts to write instructions that interact directly with the CPU, memory, and other hardware components. The precise control afforded by assembly language is a double-edged sword; while it offers immense power and flexibility, it also requires a deep understanding of the underlying machine architecture.

The Role of Assembly in Cybersecurity ### 1. Malware Analysis

One of the most prominent applications of assembly language in cybersecurity is malware analysis. Cybersecurity analysts often dissect malicious software to understand how it operates, what vulnerabilities it exploits, and how to mitigate its effects. Assembly language is essential in this process for the following reasons:

Deep Inspection: Malware often disguises its operations through obfuscation techniques. By analyzing the binary code via assembly language, security professionals can uncover hidden functionalities and behaviors.

Understanding Exploits: Many exploits target specific vulnerabilities in software. Assembly allows analysts to pinpoint the exact instructions that can lead to an exploit, enabling them to develop patches and countermeasures effectively.

2. Exploit Development

While the ethical lines can blur, the knowledge of assembly can also be employed to develop exploits for testing defenses. Security professionals and penetration testers utilize assembly to create exploits that mimic the techniques used by adversaries. This practice helps organizations identify and remediate vulnerabilities before they can be exploited maliciously.

Buffer Overflow Exploits: Many modern using assembly code for dynamic input systems require an understanding of how data is managed in memory. Exploiting buffer overflow vulnerabilities often involves writing payloads in assembly, ensuring the attacker has control over the execution flow.

Shellcode Creation: Shellcode, a small piece of code used as the payload in a vulnerability exploitation, is predominantly written in assembly. By crafting shellcode, security experts can simulate real-world attack scenarios, test defenses, and measure the effectiveness of their security posture.

3. Reverse Engineering

Reverse engineering is another domain where assembly language shines. When faced with an executable file, security analysts often need to decompile and analyze it to understand its functionality. Using assembly language is invaluable in this context for several reasons:

Recreating Logic: Many high-level constructs do not translate directly back into understandable code. Assembly language provides a way to recreate the logic used in an application's original implementation, allowing for a better understanding of its intentions.

Identifying Vulnerabilities: Understanding how an application functions at a lower level can reveal security flaws that would not be apparent in higher-level analyses.

4. Writing Custom Security Tools

Cybersecurity professionals often require tailor-made tools, whether to automate analysis, generate reports, or monitor system behavior for anomalies. The flexibility of assembly language allows practitioners to develop these tools focused on the unique needs of their environment.

Performance and Efficiency: Assembly language enables developers to write highly optimized code, making tools faster and less resource-intensive—crucial traits when monitoring vast systems for security incidents.

Creating Lightweight Agents: For scenarios where minimal intrusion is necessary, assembly language allows the development of lightweight security agents that can monitor systems with minimal overhead.

Reasons for Embracing Assembly Language

While the benefits of assembly in cybersecurity are clear, the choice to adopt its use is not without challenges. Below are compelling reasons for cybersecurity professionals to embrace assembly language despite its steeper learning curve:

Enhanced Understanding of Systems: A deeper knowledge of assembly contributes to a comprehensive understanding of how systems operate, which is vital in identifying weaknesses and creating robust cybersecurity measures.

Combat Sophisticated Threats: As cyber threats grow more sophisticated, so too must the responses. Assembly language offers the granularity needed to address these advanced threats effectively.

Prepare for Evolving Trends: With the rise of IoT, embedded systems, and hardware-based attacks, knowledge of assembly language becomes increasingly essential. Many of these devices require understanding their low-level instructions to secure effectively.

The power of assembly language in the realm of cybersecurity is undeniable. Its capacity to enhance malware analysis, reverse engineering, exploit creation, and tool development provides an indispensable arsenal for cybersecurity professionals.

Chapter 2: The Assembly Language Fundamentals

Each CPU architecture possesses its unique assembly language that reflects its register structure, instruction set, and overall design. This chapter explores the essential components of assembly language, its syntax, and its operational paradigms.

Basics of Assembly Language

2.1 What is Assembly Language?

At its core, assembly language is a low-level programming language that utilizes mnemonic codes to represent machine-level instructions. These mnemonics are symbolic representations of the binary instructions that a CPU executes. For instance, in x86 assembly language, `MOV` is used to move data from one location to another, while `ADD` performs addition.

2.2 The Role of Assemblers

An assembler is a specialized software tool that translates assembly language code into machine code, which the processor can execute directly. This translation process involves converting the mnemonics into their corresponding binary opcodes and resolving addresses for any variables or labels used.

Assemblers can vary in sophistication; some are simple one-pass assemblers that do a straightforward conversion from source code to machine code, while others are multi-pass assemblers that may perform label resolution and optimizations.

2.3 Structure of Assembly Language Programs

An assembly language program is structured in a format that offers clarity and organization. Typically, an assembly program consists of:

Labels: These are used to mark locations in the code or memory. Labels act as references that can be used for jumps or loops.

Mnemonics: The actual instructions that the CPU will execute.

Operands: These are the data or memory addresses the instructions will work with.

Directives: These are commands to the assembler itself and do not generate machine code. They instruct the assembler how to process the program (e.g., `.data` for a data segment or `.text` for code).

Example Structure

Here's a simple assembly language program that demonstrates these components:

```assembly
section .data ; Data segment
msg db 'Hello, World!', 0 ; Define a string variable
section .text ; Code segment
global _start ; Entry point for the program
_start:; Start of the program
; Write the message to stdout mov rax, 1 ; syscall: write
mov rdi, 1          ; file descriptor: stdout mov rsi, msg
                ; pointer to message mov rdx, 13
            ; number of bytes syscall   ; make syscall
```

; Exit the program

```
mov rax, 60          ; syscall: exit xor rdi, rdi     ; exit code
0 syscall        ; make syscall
```
` ` `

In this example:

The `.data` section defines a string with the null terminator.

The `.text` section contains the executable instructions.

The program makes system calls to output the message and then exit cleanly. ## Addressing Modes

One of the critical aspects of assembly language programming is understanding addressing modes, which dictate how the operands for instructions are specified. Different CPU architectures may support various addressing modes, but some common ones include:

Immediate Addressing: The operand is specified directly in the instruction (e.g., `MOV AX, 5`).

Register Addressing: The operand is located in a processor register (e.g., `MOV AX, BX`).

Direct Addressing: The instruction specifies a direct memory address (e.g., `MOV AX, [1234h]`).

Indirect Addressing: The address of the operand is stored in a register (e.g., `MOV AX, [BX]`).

Indexed Addressing: Combines a base address in a register with an offset (e.g., `MOV AX, [BX+SI]`).

Base-Offset Addressing: A combination of a base register and a constant offset.

Understanding these addressing modes is crucial for efficient memory management and optimization in assembly language programming.

Control Flow

Control flow instructions manage how the program executes in a non-linear fashion through the use of branching and looping mechanisms. Common control flow instructions in assembly include:

Jump Instructions (JMP): Unconditional jumps to a specified label.

Conditional Jumps (JE, JNE, JL, etc.): Jumps that occur based on the status flags set by previous instructions, allowing for conditional execution.

Call and Return Instructions: These are used for function calls and returns, enabling structured programming approaches.

Example of a simple loop in assembly:

```assembly
mov cx, 10     ; Set loop counter
loop_start:
; Do something
dec cx ; Decrement counter
jnz loop_start ; Jump to loop_start if cx is not zero
```

Understanding labels, mnemonics, addressing modes, and control flow structures are crucial for anyone looking to delve into the world of assembly programming.

Architecture and CPU Fundamentals

The architecture of a computer system serves as a foundation for understanding how various components interact to process information. At the heart of this architecture lies the Central Processing Unit (CPU), often dubbed the brain of the computer. This chapter delves into the fundamental concepts of computer architecture and the crucial role of the CPU, exploring their design, functionality, and evolution.

1. Understanding Computer Architecture

Computer architecture encompasses the specification and design of a computer's fundamental operational structure. It includes the physical components, such as hardware, as well as the logical structuring of these components. The essential elements of computer architecture can be categorized into three main domains:

1.1 Instruction Set Architecture (ISA)

The Instruction Set Architecture defines the set of instructions that a CPU can execute. It provides the interface between software and hardware, determining how a programmer can control the machine. ISAs can be broadly classified into two types:

Complex Instruction Set Computing (CISC): CISC architectures offer a rich set of instructions, allowing for complex operations to be performed with a single instruction. Examples include x86 architecture used in most personal computers.

Reduced Instruction Set Computing (RISC): RISC architectures simplify the instruction set, emphasizing a smaller number of simple instructions that can be executed within a single clock cycle. ARM architecture is a salient example, widely used in mobile devices.

1.2 Microarchitecture

Microarchitecture refers to the implementation of the ISA. It details how a particular ISA is realized in terms of data paths, control units, and memory hierarchies. Variants of a single ISA can have different microarchitectures. Key factors influencing microarchitecture design include:

Pipelining: This allows multiple instruction stages to be executed simultaneously, improving the throughput and efficiency of the CPU.

Superscalar Architecture: This permits the CPU to execute more than one instruction in a given clock cycle by having multiple execution units.

Multi-core and Multi-threading Designs: As processing demands increased, the industry shifted towards multi-core processors, allowing for concurrent processing by leveraging multiple cores.

1.3 System Design

This encompasses all components working with the CPU to create a complete computing system. It includes memory hierarchies (Cache, RAM, storage), input/output devices, and the communication between them.

Understanding these relationships is critical for

optimizing performance. ## 2. The CPU: Structure and Functionality

The CPU's design has evolved dramatically over the decades, but its primary functions remain consistent: fetching instructions, decoding them, executing operations, and writing back results.

2.1 Core Components of the CPU

Arithmetic Logic Unit (ALU): This component performs all arithmetic and logical operations. It's the calculator within the CPU that handles operations like addition, subtraction, and comparisons.

Control Unit (CU): The control unit orchestrates the execution of instructions by directing the operation of the ALU, memory, and I/O devices. It ensures that instructions are executed in the proper sequence and manages data flow within the CPU.

Registers: Registers are small, fast storage locations within the CPU that hold data temporarily during processing. They are utilized for immediate operations and play a significant role in enhancing CPU performance.

Cache Memory: Designed for high-speed data access, cache memory stores frequently accessed data and instructions, reducing the time it takes for the CPU to retrieve them. The cache hierarchy typically consists of L1, L2, and L3 caches, with L1 being the smallest and fastest.

2.2 The CPU Execution Cycle

The operation of the CPU can be described through the fetch-decode-execute cycle:

Fetch: The CPU retrieves an instruction from

memory, typically from RAM, using the Program Counter (PC) to track the address of the next instruction.

Decode: The fetched instruction is decoded by the control unit to determine which operation needs to be performed and which operands are involved.

Execute: The ALU performs the necessary operations based on the decoded instruction, with data provided from registers or memory.

Write Back: The results of the execution are written back to a register or memory as needed, allowing the next instruction to process subsequently.

This cycle repeats, forming the continuous processing loop that allows computers to execute complex tasks. ## 3. Evolution of CPU Technology

Over the years, the CPU has seen significant advancements driven by the continuous pursuit of higher performance and efficiency. Key developments include:

Integration and Miniaturization: Early CPUs comprised multiple discrete components; advancement in semiconductor technology enabled the integration of millions of transistors onto a single chip, fostering the development of microprocessors.

Clock Speeds and Performance: The race for faster clock speeds has driven design innovations, though limitations in heat dissipation and energy consumption led to a focus on parallelism and multi-core designs.

Energy Efficiency: As concerns about energy consumption grew in data centers and mobile devices,

CPU designs increasingly prioritize performance-per-watt, leading to the development of low-power architectures for portable computing.

Understanding computer architecture and CPU fundamentals reveals the intricate interplay between hardware and software that underpins modern computing. As technology continues to evolve, knowledge of these concepts remains essential for anyone engaged in computer science, engineering, or information technology.

Key Assembly Instructions and Operations

Cyber security threats are evolving daily, demanding robust response strategies and preventive measures. Among the foundational elements of cyber security is the concept of key assembly and operations, which forms the backbone of cryptographic systems. In this chapter, we will delve into the importance of cryptographic keys, the various types of keys, and the steps necessary to assemble, manage, and operate them effectively to ensure a secure digital environment.

1. Understanding Cryptographic Keys

Cryptographic keys are essential for encrypting and decrypting information. They act as a secret code that allows data to be securely shared between trusted entities. Keys can be symmetric or asymmetric:

Symmetric Keys: In symmetric encryption, the same key is used for both encryption and decryption. This method is faster and efficient for processing large amounts of data but requires a secure method to share the key between parties.

Asymmetric Keys: Asymmetric encryption uses a pair of keys—a public key, which can be shared openly, and a private key, which is kept secret. This model enhances security but is generally slower than symmetric encryption.

Both types of keys are crucial for securing communications, protecting sensitive information, and authenticating users.

2. Key Assembly Instructions ### 2.1 Generating Secure Keys

Use a High-Entropy Source: Keys should be generated using a high-entropy source to ensure unpredictability. This can be achieved through hardware randomness generators or cryptographically secure pseudo-random number generators (CSPRNGs).

Specify Key Length: The key length is critical for security. Longer keys provide greater security but may require more processing power. Follow industry standards:

AES (Advanced Encryption Standard): 128, 192, or 256 bits

RSA (Rivest-Shamir-Adleman): Minimum of 2048 bits

Key Format: Define the key format (hexadecimal, base64, etc.) according to system requirements.

Key Lifecycle Management: Outline the key lifecycle, including creation, storage, usage, rotation, and destruction. Proper management prevents unauthorized access and enhances security.

2.2 Storing Keys Securely

Use Secure Hardware: Store cryptographic keys in hardware security modules (HSMs) or secure enclaves that provide physical and logical security against unauthorized access.

Key Vaults: Employ key management solutions or vaults that offer encryption, access controls, and audit logs for better tracking of key use.

Backup Solutions: Ensure there are secure and encrypted backups of cryptographic keys to prevent data loss.

Access Controls: Implement strict access control policies, ensuring only authorized personnel can access cryptographic keys.

2.3 Implementing Key Distribution

Public Key Infrastructure (PKI): For asymmetric key distribution, employ a PKI to manage digital certificates and provide a secure method for key exchange.

Secure Channels: Use secure communication protocols (e.g., TLS/SSL) to transmit keys, preventing interception during transfer.

Key Sharing Agreements: If sharing symmetric keys, develop formal agreements that detail sharing protocols and enforce confidentiality.

3. Key Operations

3.1 Encryption and Decryption

Encryption Process: Describe the steps for encrypting

data with symmetric or asymmetric keys, detailing the algorithms used and the key input requirements.

Decryption Process: Provide a clear process for decrypting data, emphasizing the importance of using the correct corresponding key.

3.2 Key Rotation and Expiration

Regular Rotation: Implement a key rotation policy, conducting regular updates of cryptographic keys to mitigate risks from potential key compromise.

Expiration Policies: Establish key expiration dates and protocols for seamlessly replacing old keys, ensuring uninterrupted access to encrypted data.

3.3 Auditing and Monitoring

Logging: Maintain comprehensive logs of key usage and access, enabling accountability and facilitating audits.

Anomaly Detection: Implement monitoring systems to detect unusual access patterns related to key usage, informing of possible security breaches.

Effective management of cryptographic keys is vital in establishing trust and security in digital communications and transactions. By following best practices in key assembly instructions and operations, organizations can create resilient architectures capable of withstanding cyber threats. Properly implemented cryptographic key strategies not only protect sensitive data but also enhance an organization's credibility and compliance with regulatory standards.

Chapter 3: Memory Management and Assembly

This chapter delves into the intricacies of memory management and the role of assembly language, exploring how they interrelate, their significance in system performance, and the strategies employed to optimize memory utilization.

3.1 Understanding Memory Management ### 3.1.1 What is Memory Management?

Memory management refers to the processes that handle a computer's memory allocation and deallocation. It encompasses the methods through which a computer system keeps track of each byte in a computer's memory. This includes the physical memory (RAM) and virtual memory – a portion of the disk that appears as if it were a part of the RAM.

Efficient memory management is crucial for any operating system (OS) because it maximizes performance and ensures that programs run smoothly without running into memory leaks or corrupting data due to improper access.

3.1.2 Memory Organization

Memory is typically organized into a hierarchy to balance cost and access speed. At the top of this hierarchy is the CPU cache, followed by main memory (RAM), and finally secondary storage (like hard drives and SSDs). Understanding this hierarchy allows developers to write more efficient programs by optimizing how data is accessed and stored.

3.1.3 Functions of Memory Management Memory

management serves several key functions:

Allocation and Deallocation: It allocates memory blocks to processes when requested and frees the memory when it is no longer needed. The methods used can vary from static allocation (fixed size) to dynamic allocation (flexible size).

Address Translation: Modern operating systems often implement virtual memory systems where memory addresses used by programs are translated to physical addresses in RAM. This provides an abstraction layer that allows programs to use more memory than is physically available.

Memory Protection: It ensures that processes do not interfere with each other's memory, maintaining system stability and security.

Garbage Collection: In higher-level languages, garbage collection is an automated process of reclaiming memory that is no longer in use, helping to prevent memory leaks.

3.2 The Role of Assembly Language ### 3.2.1 What is Assembly Language?

Assembly language is a low-level programming language that is closely related to machine code. Each assembly language is specific to a computer architecture, providing a set of symbolic names and a syntax for the machine instructions that a CPU can execute.

Assembly plays a critical role in system programming and in situations where performance is paramount because it gives programmers fine-grained control over hardware resources.

3.2.2 Characteristics of Assembly Language

Hardware Dependence: Different CPUs have different assembly languages. Understanding the target architecture is essential for writing effective assembly code.

Performance: Assembly language allows developers to write highly optimized code that can outperform high-level languages, especially in resource-constrained environments.

Direct Memory Access: Programmers have the ability to directly manipulate memory addresses, enabling precise control over data structures and allocation strategies.

3.2.3 Assembly Language in Memory Management

Assembly language is often used in system-level programming tasks, including memory management:

Memory Allocation: Using assembly, a programmer can implement custom memory allocators, taking care to manage how memory is allocated and freed manually. This can lead to optimized performance for specific applications.

Memory Mapping: Assembly language allows for direct manipulation of page tables and other structures used by the OS for managing memory spaces, enabling detailed control over how memory is accessed and transferred.

Profiling and Optimization: Assembly can be used to profile the performance of memory accesses and optimize hot spots in code that deal with memory allocation and data access.

3.3 Combining Memory Management and Assembly Language

In practice, memory management systems use a combination of higher-level language features and low-level assembly instructions to optimize performance. Operating systems like Linux use C, which compiles down to assembly, allowing developers to write performance-critical components in assembly while still benefiting from the more accessible features of C.

3.3.1 Case Study: Linux Memory Management

The Linux kernel employs a sophisticated memory management scheme that involves techniques like paging, segmentation, and demand paging. Developers can write assembly routines for the kernel that handle low-level tasks like page swapping and interrupt handling, ensuring that the memory system functions efficiently.

3.3.2 Best Practices for Memory Management in Assembly

When writing assembly code that involves memory management, developers should adhere to several best practices:

Minimize Fragmentation: By carefully planning memory allocation patterns, programmers can decrease memory fragmentation, which helps maintain an efficient memory pool.

Use Appropriate Data Structures: Choosing the right data structure in assembly for the intended task can save memory space and improve access time.

Implement Thorough Testing: Memory bugs can be particularly challenging to diagnose. Rigorously testing assembly code that involves memory management is essential to ensure reliability and correctness.

Memory management and assembly language are integral components of low-level programming that offer developers unique capabilities and challenges. A solid understanding of memory management principles enhances the ability to write efficient assembly code, which in turn can leverage the full power of hardware resources.

Memory Layout and Stack Handling

Understanding memory layout and stack handling is fundamental to mastering assembly language and low-level programming. Memory in modern computer systems is organized in a structured way that facilitates efficient data management and execution of programs. This chapter will delve into the critical components of memory layout, including the stack, heap, and data segments, and how to manipulate these areas effectively using assembly language.

1. Memory Layout

1.1 Organization of Memory

The memory of a typical computer system is organized into several segments:

Text Segment: This segment contains the compiled machine code of the program. It is typically read- only to prevent accidental modification while running.

Data Segment: The data segment holds initialized and uninitialized global and static variables. It is divided into two parts:

Initialized Data Segment: Stores variables that are initialized with a value.

BSS Segment (Block Started by Symbol): Stores variables that are declared but not initialized.

Heap: The heap is a region used for dynamic memory allocation during program execution. Memory here can be allocated and deallocated as needed, which is essential for creating structures like linked lists, trees, and dynamically sized arrays.

Stack: The stack is used for managing function calls and local variables. It operates on a Last In, First Out (LIFO) principle, meaning that the most recently added data is the first to be removed. The stack grows downwards in memory, starting from a high address.

1.2 Memory Addressing

In assembly language, memory is accessed using specific address values. These addresses can be absolute or relative:

Absolute Addressing: Accesses a specific address in memory directly. For instance, using a specific register or an immediate value.

Relative Addressing: Accesses memory location based on an offset from a specific base address, commonly used in conjunction with pointers and the stack.

2. Stack Handling ### 2.1 Stack Operations

The stack supports several fundamental operations:

Push: This operation adds a value to the top of the stack. In assembly, it is often performed using the

`PUSH` instruction.

Pop: This operation removes the value from the top of the stack. It can be executed using the `POP` instruction.

Call: This instruction adds the return address to the stack before jumping to the target function.

Ret: This instruction retrieves the return address from the stack, facilitating a jump back to the calling function.

2.2 Function Calls and Returns

When a function is called, the following occurs:

The current instruction pointer (EIP/RIP) is pushed onto the stack to save the return address.

Space for local variables is allocated on the stack (by adjusting the stack pointer).

Parameters may be pushed onto the stack, depending on the calling convention being used.

The function executes its code.

Upon completion, the function might return a value that can be stored in a designated register.

When `RET` is executed, the previously saved instruction pointer is popped from the stack, and control is returned to the calling function.

2.3 Local Variables and Scope

Local variables are stored on the stack and have a limited scope, meaning they only exist during the function's execution. When the function returns, the stack pointer is adjusted to free up space, effectively destroying any local variables. The memory for these local variables is reclaimed and can be reused by subsequent function calls.

2.4 Stack Overflow and Underflow

Care must be taken when manipulating the stack to avoid stack overflow (exceeding the allocated memory for the stack) or stack underflow (performing a pop operation without sufficient data on the stack). Both conditions can lead to unpredictable behavior and program crashes.

3. Assembly Language Example

To illustrate stack handling and memory layout, let's consider a simple assembly program that calculates the factorial of a number using recursion.

```assembly
```assembly section .text global _start

_start:

mov ebx, 5    ; Factorial of 5 call factorial

; Now ebx contains the factorial result

; Exit the program

mov eax, 1    ; syscall: exit

xor ebx, ebx  ; return 0 int 0x80

factorial:

; Base case: if n <= 1 return 1

cmp ebx, 1 jle .base_case
```
```

```
; Recursive case: n * factorial(n - 1) push ebx    ; Save n on
the stack

dec ebx        ; n - 1

call factorial  ; Recursive call

pop ebx        ; Restore n from the stack

; Multiply the result by n

imul eax, ebx ; eax = n * factorial(n - 1) ret

.base_case:

mov eax, 1     ; Return 1 ret
```
` ` `

Explanation of the Code:

_start: The program begins execution here. It sets up the base number for factorial calculation and calls the function.

Calling factorial: The number to compute the factorial is passed by storing it in the EBX register. The result will be returned in the EAX register.

factorial function: This function handles both the base case and recursive case. It uses `PUSH` and

`POP` to manage the stack and saves the state of the EBX register for recursive calls.

Returning values: The calculated factorial is returned in the EAX register.

Understanding how the stack operates, how to manipulate memory segments, and the scope of local variables empowers programmers to write efficient and reliable low-level code. Mastery of these concepts aids in debugging, optimization, and leveraging capabilities in advanced programming domains such as operating systems, embedded systems, and system-level applications.

Register and Stack Manipulation in Assembly

Understanding registers and the stack is crucial for efficient programming and manipulating data at a fine level of detail. This chapter aims to introduce the fundamental concepts of registers and stack manipulation in assembly, illustrating how these elements work together to manage data and control flow in programs.

1. Understanding Registers

Registers are small storage locations within the CPU that hold data temporarily during processing. They are faster than accessing main memory and are essential for executing instructions. Different architectures have different registers, but most include general-purpose registers (GPRs), special-purpose registers, and status registers.

1.1 General-Purpose Registers

General-purpose registers can be used for a variety of functions, including storing operands, holding temporary data, or indicating addresses. For example, in the x86 architecture, common general-purpose registers include:

EAX: Accumulator for arithmetic operations.

EBX: Base register used for data storage.

ECX: Counter for loops and string operations.

EDX: Data register, often used in conjunction with EAX for arithmetic. ### 1.2 Special-Purpose Registers

These registers serve specific functions that are vital for the control of the CPU:

Instruction Pointer (EIP/RIP): Points to the next instruction to be executed.

Stack Pointer (ESP/RSP): Points to the current top of the stack.

Base Pointer (EBP/RBP): Used to reference parameters and local variables in the stack frame. ### 1.3 Status Register

The status register contains flags that indicate the status of the processor, such as the Zero Flag (ZF), Sign Flag (SF), and Carry Flag (CF). These flags are crucial for controlling program flow based on comparison operations.

2. The Stack

The stack is a region of memory that operates in a Last In, First Out (LIFO) manner. It is typically used for storing temporary data, passing parameters to functions, and saving the return address during function calls. The stack grows downwards in many architectures, meaning that when you push data onto the stack, the stack pointer decreases.

2.1 Stack Operations

The two primary operations on the stack are **push** and **pop**:

Push: This operation places data onto the stack and decrements the stack pointer. For example, in x86 assembly, the instruction `PUSH EAX` decreases the stack pointer and stores the contents of the EAX register at the new location pointed by the stack pointer.

Pop: This operation removes data from the stack and increments the stack pointer. For instance, `POP EAX` retrieves the top value from the stack and restores the stack pointer to its previous state.

2.2 Function Calls and Return Addresses

In most assembly languages, when a function is called, the return address is automatically pushed onto the stack. This allows the program to return to the correct location after the function execution is complete. The common sequence for a function call generally looks like this:

Push the return address onto the stack.

Execute the function, performing operations and using the stack for local variables.

Return control to the caller using the `RET` instruction, which pops the return address off the stack and jumps to that address.

3. Stack Frames

When functions are called, a stack frame is created for each invocation. This frame consists of the return address, parameters, and local variables. Proper management of stack frames is essential for recursive functions and maintaining parameter integrity across multiple layers of function calls.

3.1 Setting Up a Stack Frame

In x86 assembly, setting up a stack frame typically involves:

Pushing the base pointer (EBP): This saves the previous frame pointer.

Setting the base pointer to the current stack pointer (ESP): This establishes a new frame of reference.

Allocating space for local variables: This can be done by decrementing ESP by the number of bytes required for the local variables.

A typical sequence looks like this:

```assembly
PUSH EBP    ; Save the old base pointer

MOV EBP, ESP            ; Establish the new base
pointer SUB ESP, 16; Allocate space for local variables
```

3.2 Cleaning Up a Stack Frame

When the function completes, it's vital to restore the previous stack frame. This involves:

Moving the base pointer back to its original value.

Restoring the stack pointer.

Returning to the caller.

Here's how that would be implemented:

```assembly
MOV ESP, EBP            ; Restore the original stack
pointer POP EBP    ; Restore the old base pointer

RET    ; Return to the caller
```

4. Practical Examples

4.1 Simple Function Example

Let's implement a simple assembly program to illustrate the concepts of registers and stack manipulation through a function that adds two numbers.

```assembly
section .text global _start

_start:

; Call the function with parameters 5 and 10 PUSH 10

PUSH 5

CALL add_numbers

ADD ESP, 8   ; Clean up the parameters from stack

; Exit program (Linux syscall) MOV EAX, 1      ;    syscall: exit MOV EBX, 0     ; status: 0 INT 0x80

add_numbers:

PUSH EBP   ; Save the old base pointer MOV EBP, ESP   ; Establish new base pointer

; Parameters are on the stack

MOV EAX, [EBP + 8]  ; First parameter

ADD EAX, [EBP + 12] ; Add second parameter

MOV ESP, EBP   ; Restore the stack pointer POP EBP   ; Restore the old base pointer RET      ;    Return with the sum in EAX
```

4.2 Recursive Function Example

Recursion can be elegantly handled by the stack, as each

47

function call creates a new frame. Here's a simple recursive function to calculate the factorial of a number.

```assembly factorial:
; Base case: If n is 0, return 1 CMP EAX, 0

JE base_case

; Recursive case: n * factorial(n - 1) PUSH EAX  ; Save n

DEC EAX     ; Calculate n - 1 CALL factorial  ; Recursive call POP EAX        ; Restore n

IMUL EAX, EAX   ; Multiply EAX by the return value RET base_case:

MOV EAX, 1 ; Return 1 for factorial(0) RET
```

Manipulating registers and the stack effectively is fundamental for writing efficient and robust assembly language programs. Understanding how to push and pop data as well as manage stack frames is crucial for function calls, local variables, and parameter passing.

Chapter 4: Reverse Engineering with Assembly

This chapter will guide you through the essentials of assembly language, tools and techniques for reverse engineering, and practical applications in enhancing security.

4.1 Understanding Assembly Language

Assembly language serves as a bridge between high-level programming languages and machine code. Each assembly instruction corresponds closely to machine code, making it a low-level language that offers unprecedented control over hardware and system resources. Furthermore, each CPU architecture has its own assembly language, which means it's vital to have a good grasp of the specific language being used when performing reverse engineering.

4.1.1 Importance of Assembly in Cyber Security

Reverse engineering often involves analyzing binaries compiled from higher-level languages into machine code. Understanding assembly allows cybersecurity professionals to:

Dissect Malicious Code: By translating machine instructions back into human-readable form, security experts can better understand the logic behind malware behavior and its methods of exploitation.

Vulnerability Research: Determine how software vulnerabilities arise in conjunction with how the code interacts with memory and system resources.

Exploit Development: Craft exploits by modifying

assembly instructions, allowing practitioners to understand how an application can be manipulated.

4.2 Tools for Reverse Engineering

To successfully reverse engineer software, a set of tools is essential. The following tools are popular among security professionals for their effectiveness and versatility in handling different binary formats and architectures.

4.2.1 Disassemblers

Disassemblers convert machine code into assembly language. Examples include:

IDA Pro: A powerful, interactive disassembler that provides extensive features for analyzing binaries.

Ghidra: A free, open-source tool developed by the NSA that includes disassembly and decompilation features.

4.2.2 Debuggers

Debuggers are useful for stepping through the code execution in real-time. Some commonly used debuggers include:

GDB: The GNU Debugger is a versatile tool for debugging applications running on Unix-like systems.

OllyDbg: A popular debugger for Windows binaries, especially useful for analyzing malware. ### 4.2.3 Hex Editors

Hex editors provide a means to view and edit binary files at a byte-level. They are essential for modifying binaries directly. Examples include:

HxD: A fast hex editor for Windows that offers

comprehensive features.

Hex Fiend: A macOS application designed for large file sizes and built for efficiency. ## 4.3 Basic Techniques in Reverse Engineering

4.3.1 Static Analysis

Static analysis involves examining the code without executing it. This step often includes:

Identifying Import Tables: Understanding the external functions a binary depends upon can give insight into its behavior.

Reading Control Flow: Analyzing how the function calls and jumps interact can reveal the program's high-level operations.

Extracting Strings: Human-readable strings often reveal clues about the functionality, user interfaces, or hidden URLs.

4.3.2 Dynamic Analysis

Dynamic analysis involves running the binary in a controlled environment. This method allows auditors to observe runtime behavior and interactions with the system:

Setting Breakpoints: Pausing execution at critical points provides insight into program flow and variable states.

Memory Analysis: Observing how the binary manipulates memory helps to identify buffer overflows and other vulnerabilities.

4.4 Practical Applications of Reverse Engineering

4.4.1 Malware Analysis

Given the ever-growing threat of malware, reverse engineering is pivotal in understanding and mitigating attacks. Analysts can unpack complex malware, uncover its payload, and develop signature-based detection methods.

4.4.2 Security Audits

Security audits often involve reviewing binaries for vulnerabilities. By reverse engineering proprietary code, security experts can identify potential security flaws before they are exploited by malicious actors.

4.4.3 License Key Generation

In some cases, reverse engineering is used to develop license key generators for legitimate software that has protective measures against unauthorized use. This practice can help companies assess their product security.

4.5 Ethical Considerations

It's crucial to note that while reverse engineering has numerous legitimate applications in cyber security, it straddles a fine line regarding legality and ethics. Understanding licensing agreements, intellectual property rights, and complying with local laws are imperative to practice reverse engineering responsibly.

Reverse engineering with assembly language is an indispensable technique in the arsenal of cybersecurity professionals. By enabling deep insight into software behavior, it equips experts to tackle current and future cyber threats more effectively.

Tools and Techniques for Reverse Engineering

This chapter explores various tools and techniques used in reverse engineering, particularly within the context of assembly language, and highlights their application in cybersecurity.

1. Understanding Reverse Engineering

Before delving into the tools and techniques, it's essential to define reverse engineering. Reverse engineering is the process of deconstructing a software application to analyze its components and understand how it operates. This can involve examining code, understanding algorithms, and identifying potential security flaws. In cybersecurity, reverse engineering is commonly used to analyze malware, check for vulnerabilities in software, and secure systems against potential exploits.

1.1 The Role of Assembly Language

Assembly language serves as a bridge between high-level programming languages and machine code. It provides a more human-readable format of the binary instructions executed by a CPU. Understanding assembly is crucial because many programs ultimately run as machine code, and reverse engineers must be able to read and interpret this low-level representation to analyze behavior and functionality.

2. Tools for Reverse Engineering

Several tools assist in the reverse engineering process, each with unique features well-suited for analysis at the assembly language level. Below are some widely used tools in the cybersecurity community.

2.1 Disassemblers

Disassemblers convert machine code back into assembly language, which can be studied by analysts.

Ghidra: An open-source tool developed by the NSA, Ghidra features an interactive user interface, boasts robust analysis capabilities, and supports various architectures. Its functionality includes code analysis and graphing features that aid in visualizing control flows.

IDA Pro: The Interactive DisAssembler (IDA) is a commercial tool renowned for its powerful capabilities in code analysis. IDA Pro allows for detailed manual inspections and provides plugins for enhanced functionality.

2.2 Debuggers

Debuggers are essential for analyzing how a program executes in real-time, allowing for a deeper understanding of program behavior.

OllyDbg: This 32-bit assembler-level debugger is crucial for analyzing binary code. It allows for dynamic analysis and supports breakpoints, making it a favorite among malware analysts.

x64dbg: An open-source debugger designed for both x86 and x64 binaries, x64dbg offers an organized interface and numerous built-in functions that assist in tracking program execution and altering its state.

2.3 Binary Analysis Tools

Binary analysis tools provide features to analyze the structure and contents of binary files.

Radare2: A robust framework for binary analysis, Radare2 provides tools for viewing, analyzing, and patching binaries. Its command-line interface requires a learning curve but offers flexible and powerful capabilities.

Binary Ninja: This commercial tool leverages a combination of a powerful disassembler and a user-friendly interface. With built-in analysis features and API access for customization, it appeals to both newcomers and experienced analysts.

3. Techniques in Reverse Engineering

After selecting appropriate tools, various techniques can be employed in the reverse engineering process. Understanding these techniques is vital in identifying vulnerabilities and threats.

3.1 Static Analysis

Static analysis involves analyzing the binary without executing it. This can include examining the disassembled code, looking for known vulnerabilities, or extracting strings that might reveal significant information about the program's behavior.

3.2 Dynamic Analysis

Dynamic analysis entails executing the program in a controlled environment and observing its behavior. This can help uncover runtime vulnerabilities, such as buffer overflows or unauthorized access. This technique may also involve the use of sandbox environments to safely execute potentially harmful software.

3.3 Behavioral Analysis

This technique monitors how software interacts with the

operating system and other programs. By understanding API calls, file access, and network communications, cybersecurity professionals can create a profile of the software and identify exploits.

3.4 Patching and Modifying

After identifying vulnerabilities through reverse engineering, the next logical step is patching or modifying the code to eliminate risks. This can involve altering assembly instructions to change the flow of execution, remove unwanted features, or address security flaws.

4. Ethical Considerations

While reverse engineering is a powerful tool for cybersecurity, it is essential to operate within ethical and legal boundaries. Many software licenses prohibit reverse engineering, and unauthorized access to proprietary code can lead to legal repercussions. Cybersecurity professionals should ensure they have permission or are operating within applicable laws when performing reverse engineering activities.

In the realm of cybersecurity, the ability to reverse engineer software at the assembly language level is invaluable. Tools such as Ghidra, IDA Pro, OllyDbg, and Radare2 equip analysts with the capabilities to dissect and understand the complexities of binary code.

Analyzing Executables with Disassemblers

One of the most effective methods for dissecting executable files is through disassembly, a technique that translates binary code into a human-readable assembly language. This chapter aims to provide a comprehensive overview of disassemblers, their operational mechanisms, and their relevance to cybersecurity.

1. Understanding Executables

At its core, an executable file is a compiled version of source code that can be directly executed by a computer's operating system. These files contain machine code tailored for a specific architecture, often making them opaque to users and security analysts. The complexity of modern executables stems from various factors, including optimization by compilers and the inclusion of different code sections (text, data, stack, heap). Therefore, tools are needed to reveal the underlying logic and flow of these binaries.

1.1 Anatomy of Executables

Header: Contains metadata about the executable, such as entry points, section locations, and sizes.

Code Section: Holds the compiled machine code that the CPU executes.

Data Section: Stores global variables and static data.

Import/Export Tables: Lists functions and variables imported from or exported to other binaries. ## 2. Disassemblers: Overview and Functionality

Disassemblers are specialized tools designed to convert machine code back into assembly language. Unlike decompilers, which attempt a higher-level reconstruction of the source code, disassemblers focus on breaking down the binary into assembly instructions, making it easier to analyze specific operations.

2.1 Types of Disassemblers

Static Disassemblers: Analyze the binary without executing it. They generate assembly code based solely on the binary's structure and existing patterns.

Dynamic Disassemblers: Work alongside a debugger to analyze the executable while it runs, allowing the analyst to view execution at runtime.

2.2 Popular Disassemblers

IDA Pro: A powerful tool favored in the security community for its advanced functionality, graphing capabilities, and support for numerous architectures.

Ghidra: A free, open-source disassembly suite developed by the NSA, providing robust analysis and support for plugins.

Radare2: An open-source framework offering a wealth of tools for reverse engineering and analyzing binaries.

3. The Disassembly Process

Disassembling an executable involves several systematic steps, which include loading the binary into a disassembler, navigating through its sections, and interpreting the machine code.

3.1 Initial Setup

When disassembling an executable, the first step is setting up the disassembler correctly. This includes configuring the architecture type and other parameters to ensure the tool interprets the binary correctly.

3.2 Navigating Code Sections

After loading the binary, the analyst examines the code

sections. The disassembler will present a listing of assembly instructions line-by-line, often alongside their corresponding memory addresses. By studying these instructions and their flow, the analyst can begin to piece together the executable's processes.

3.3 Understanding Control Flow

One of the critical aspects of disassembly is analyzing control flow—how the program executes various paths. Tools often visualize this flow graphically, showing jump instructions, loops, and branching.

Understanding this flow is essential for identifying potential vulnerabilities or malicious behavior. ## 4. Practical Applications in Cybersecurity

The disassembly of executables has significant implications in cybersecurity. Here are some practical applications:

4.1 Malware Analysis

Disassemblers allow analysts to dissect malware, understanding its payload, persistence mechanisms, and network activity. This intelligence aids in developing defenses against threats.

4.2 Vulnerability Research

By analyzing known vulnerable binaries, security professionals can identify exploitation vectors. Understanding how vulnerabilities manifest enables better patching and mitigation strategies.

4.3 Threat Hunting

Disassemblers facilitate the examination of suspicious executables found in user environments. By analyzing these binaries, security teams can determine if they exhibit malicious behavior or if they warrant further investigation.

5. Challenges and Limitations

While disassembling executables offers numerous advantages, analysts face several challenges:

Code Obfuscation: Malicious actors often employ obfuscation techniques to trick disassemblers, making understanding the binary more difficult.

Complexity of Modern Binaries: Modern applications may incorporate complex features like Just-In-Time (JIT) compilation, leading to further complications in accurate analysis.

By converting binaries into assembly language, disassemblers generate insights that can lead to improved security postures, effective threat detection, and better mitigations against vulnerabilities. Mastery of disassembly techniques, along with a robust understanding of assembly language, empowers analysts to defend against the ever-evolving landscape of cyber threats.

Chapter 5: Exploiting Vulnerabilities: The Buffer Overflow

This chapter delves into the intricacies of buffer overflow vulnerabilities, focusing on assembly language, where direct memory manipulation provides both power and peril.

5.1 Understanding Buffer Overflow

At its core, a buffer overflow occurs when a program writes more data to a block of memory, or "buffer," than it was allocated. This excess data can overwrite adjacent memory locations, leading to unpredictable behavior, crashes, or even the execution of malicious code. The severity of a buffer overflow is exacerbated when exploited, allowing an attacker to control the flow of execution in a program.

5.1.1 Memory Layout

To grasp buffer overflow vulnerabilities, one must first understand the memory layout of a program. In most systems, program memory is divided into several segments:

Text Segment: Contains the compiled code of the program.

Data Segment: Holds global and static variables.

Heap: Dynamically allocated memory during the program's runtime.

Stack: Used for function calls, local variables, and control flow.

Buffer overflows typically occur on the stack, where local

variables are stored. The stack grows downwards in most architectures (e.g., x86), meaning that a buffer placed higher in memory can overwrite lower memory addresses.

5.1.2 Example of Buffer Overflow

Let's consider a typical example in C that may lead to a buffer overflow. The following function reads a user-input string into a fixed-size buffer without proper bounds checking:

```c
void vulnerable_function() { char buffer[64];

gets(buffer); // Unsafe function that reads input without limit

}
```

If an attacker provides more than 64 bytes of input, the excess characters will overflow the buffer, potentially overwriting the return address of the function. This introduces the possibility of redirecting execution to arbitrary code.

5.2 Assembly Language Perspective

When a buffer overflow occurs, it's crucial to understand how this manifests at the assembly level. Let's look at the assembly equivalent of the C code above.

5.2.1 Compiling to Assembly

Using a compiler, the C function above translates to assembly language. Below is a simplified representation of what this might look like in x86 assembly:

```asm
vulnerable_function:
push ebp        ; Save base pointer
mov ebp, esp ; Establish stack frame
sub esp, 64            ; Allocate 64 bytes for the buffer call
gets    ; Read input into buffer
leave   ; Clean up stack frame
ret     ; Return from function
```

Here, `sub esp, 64` allocates space on the stack for the buffer. If an input longer than 64 bytes is provided to the `gets` function, it will overwrite the saved base pointer (EBP) and the return address on the stack.

5.3 Constructing the Exploit

Exploiting a buffer overflow involves crafting an input that will manipulate the execution flow. The following steps typically outline the exploit development process:

5.3.1 Finding the Offset

To exploit the vulnerability, an attacker first must determine the buffer's exact size and where the return address is stored. This can sometimes be done through a process called "fuzzing," sending random data and observing program behavior until crashes occur.

5.3.2 Crafting the Payload Next, the attacker crafts the payload:

Padding: Fill the buffer with non-exploiting data (NOPs or other characters) to reach the return address.

Return Address: Insert the desired return address. This is typically the location of the malicious code (often referred to as "shellcode").

Malicious Code: This is the actual code the attacker wants to execute. It often includes commands to spawn a shell or exfiltrate data.

A crafted payload might look like this in a visual format:
```

[Padding...] [Return Address] [Shellcode]
```

5.3.3 Launching the Attack

Once the payload is carefully constructed and tested, it's sent to the vulnerable program. If successful, the overflow allows the attacker to redirect execution and run the malicious payload, gaining control over the system.

5.4 Mitigation Techniques

Despite the inherent risks, there are strategies to mitigate buffer overflow vulnerabilities:

Use Safe Functions: Replace unsafe functions like `gets` with safer alternatives like `fgets`, where input size can be controlled.

Stack Canaries: Introduce guard values placed next to return addresses to detect modifications.

Address Space Layout Randomization (ASLR): Randomizes memory addresses used by system and application processes, making it harder for attackers to predict where to redirect execution.

Executable Space Protection: Ensure that stack and heap memory cannot be executed, thwarting shellcode execution.

Understanding assembly language and the details of how memory is structured and manipulated underlines the importance of writing secure code. As we advance in software development and security practices, a thorough comprehension of vulnerabilities like buffer overflows shall remain indispensable for securing systems against malicious exploitation.

Understanding Buffer Overflows in Assembly

This chapter delves into the essence of buffer overflows, particularly within the context of assembly language, elucidating their mechanics, implications, and preventive measures.

What is a Buffer Overflow?

A buffer overflow occurs when data written to a buffer exceeds its allocated limit, causing adjacent memory locations to be overwritten. A buffer, in programming, is a contiguous block of memory allocated to store data temporarily. Buffers are often used to hold strings, arrays, and other data types in languages like C and C++, which provide the flexibility of manual memory management but lack inherent bounds checking.

When vulnerable software receives user input, it may fail to validate the length of the input data adequately. As a consequence, an attacker can exploit this vulnerability by sending a specially crafted input that overflows the buffer, potentially leading to arbitrary code execution, data corruption, or crashes.

The Mechanics of Buffer Overflows in Assembly

To understand buffer overflows, one must appreciate how memory is managed at the assembly level. Within an application, areas of memory are designated for various purposes, including the stack, heap, and data segments. The stack is particularly important because it manages function calls, local variables, and control flow via a structure known as the call stack.

Stack Memory and Buffer Allocations

When functions are invoked, a stack frame is created, which includes space for local variables, saved registers, and the return address of the current function. With assembly, we can have a visual understanding of how buffers are managed:

```assembly
push ebp          ; Save old base pointer

mov ebp, esp      ; Set new base pointer

sub  esp, 0x20    ; Allocate 32 bytes for local variables
```

In this example, a buffer of 32 bytes is allocated on the stack. However, if a program does not check the amount of data written into this buffer, an attacker can supply more than 32 bytes, overflowing the buffer and overwriting important control data like the saved base pointer or the return address.

Overwriting Control Data

When we write beyond the buffer's allocated memory, we can target specific locations on the stack. For example, if a return address is located directly after our buffer and we overwrite it, the next time the function attempts to return, it will jump to whatever address we placed there. This can lead to the execution of malicious code.

Below is a simplified illustration of the stack after a buffer overflow occurs:

```
|------------------------| <--- Overflow starts here
| Local Variable (Buffer) |


|        |
| Return Address    | <    Overwritten
|        |
```

Exploiting Buffer Overflows

Let's consider a practical scenario. Suppose we have a vulnerable C function that looks like this:

```c
void vulnerable_function(char *input) { char buffer[32];
strcpy(buffer, input); // No bounds checking
```

67

```
}
```
```
` ` `
```

By calling `vulnerable_function` with a string longer than 32 bytes, an attacker can carefully craft the input to overwrite the return address. They may include machine code (shellcode) or a pointer to an existing executable code segment. Attackers often employ NOP sleds, a sequence of NOP (no operation) instructions, to enhance the likelihood of successful execution.

Preventing Buffer Overflows

Awareness is the first line of defense against buffer overflows. Here are critical strategies for prevention:

Bounds Checking: Always ensure that input length is verified before writing to a buffer. Functions like `strncpy()` in C can be used instead of `strcpy()`.

Stack Canaries: Modern compilers insert canary values next to buffers on the stack. If a buffer overflow occurs, the canary value will be altered, triggering an exception before control flow can be compromised.

Address Space Layout Randomization (ASLR): This technique randomizes memory addresses used by system and application processes, making it difficult for attackers to predict where their shellcode will be located.

Non-Executable Stack: Configuring memory segments as non-executable prevents executing code on the stack, blocking many types of attacks.

Using Safe Libraries: Leveraging secure coding libraries or languages with automatic bounds checking (e.g., Python, Rust) can eliminate many vulnerabilities inherent to assembly and C.

By understanding their workings at the assembly level, cybersecurity professionals can recognize vulnerabilities and implement strategies to mitigate risk.

Crafting Exploits for Buffer Overflow Vulnerabilities

Understanding how to exploit these vulnerabilities is crucial for both offensive and defensive cybersecurity strategies. This chapter will explore buffer overflow exploits specifically in the context of assembly language, covering the necessary concepts, techniques, and practical examples to illustrate this critical area of cybersecurity.

Understanding Buffer Overflow Vulnerabilities

A buffer overflow occurs when data that exceeds the buffer's allocated size is written to the buffer. This can corrupt adjacent memory, resulting in unintended behavior, including program crashes or the execution of malicious code. Buffer overflows often arise due to inadequate boundary checking or improper data validation in C or C++ programs, where the programmer must manage memory manually.

Anatomy of a Buffer Overflow

Memory Layout: Understanding how a program manages memory is essential. Stack memory, where local variables are stored, is particularly vulnerable. An attacker manipulates the stack frame of a function to overwrite the return address with a pointer to their own code.

Return Address Overwrite: The key to a buffer overflow exploit is overwriting the return address that gets pushed onto the stack when a function is called. Once this address is manipulated, the program will execute code located at the attacker's specified address, usually the start of a buffer they control.

Shellcode Invocation: The payload delivered via buffer overflow is often referred to as "shellcode," a piece of code that represents the attacker's command, usually designed to spawn a shell or execute arbitrary commands.

Assembly Language and Exploit Crafting

Assembly language provides a direct interface to the underlying architecture, making it a powerful tool for crafting exploits. It allows attackers to control CPU registers and manipulate memory directly, offering precise control over the exploit's execution.

Basic Concepts of Assembly Language

Registers: CPU registers are small storage locations that provide fast access to data. Manipulating these registers is crucial for controlling program flow during an exploit.

Instructions: Assembly language consists of mnemonics that correspond to machine-level instructions. Understanding these instructions is essential for writing efficient shellcode.

System Calls: Exploits often require interaction with the operating system, making system calls a common feature in shellcode.

Crafting the Exploit

Step 1: Identification of Vulnerability

Find a program that is vulnerable to buffer overflow, typically one where user input is not validated. A classic example is the use of `gets()` in C, which does not limit input size.

Step 2: Setting Up the Environment

Use a controlled test environment (e.g., a virtual machine) with debuggers (like gdb) and tools (like pwndbg) for testing and debugging.

Step 3: Generating Shellcode

Shellcode is a small piece of code used as the payload in an exploit. It needs to be written in assembly, compiled, and turned into an executable format that can be injected into the vulnerable program.

Example of a simple Linux shellcode written in assembly:

```assembly section .text
global _start
_start:
; execve("/bin/sh", NULL, NULL) xor rax, rax
mov rdi, rax push rdi
mov rdi, 0x68732f2f6e69622f ; //bin/sh shr rdi, 0x8
push rdi mov rdi, rsp xor rsi, rsi xor rdx, rdx syscall
```

This code produces a payload that launches a shell. #### Step 4: Constructing the Exploit

Now, build the exploit that will send the input to the

vulnerable program:

Payload Construction: Create a buffer that contains NOP instructions (`0x90`) leading to the shellcode. Following it, add the shellcode itself. Then, pad the input with enough bytes (NOP, shellcode) to overflow the buffer and overwrite the return address.

Determine the Return Address: Use a debugger to find the exact stack address that will be overwritten. It's often necessary to offset the buffer size and point to the start of your shellcode.

Example Python code for constructing the exploit input:

```python
import os import struct

# Setup constants

BUFFER_SIZE = 64  # Size of the vulnerable buffer

SHELLCODE_ADDRESS = 0xbffffb00  # Example address where shellcode is located # Create a payload

nop_sled = b'\x90' * (BUFFER_SIZE - len(shellcode)) # NOP sled

payload = nop_sled + shellcode + struct.pack('<I', SHELLCODE_ADDRESS)

# Execute the vulnerable program

os.system(f"echo -ne '{payload}' | ./vulnerable_program")
```

Step 5: Testing the Exploit

Run the exploit against the vulnerable application. If crafted correctly, the application should execute the shellcode, providing the attacker with a shell.

Defenses Against Buffer Overflow

Understanding how to exploit buffer overflow vulnerabilities leads naturally to discussions about defensive measures. Protection mechanisms include:

Stack Canaries: Special values placed on the stack to detect overflow attempts.

Address Space Layout Randomization (ASLR): Randomizes memory addresses to make it harder for attackers to predict where their payload resides.

Non-Executable Stack (NX): Prevents execution of code from the stack or heap, mitigating the impact of shellcode injection.

Crafting exploits for buffer overflow vulnerabilities in assembly language is a complex process that requires a deep understanding of computer architecture, programming, and security principles. While the techniques shared in this chapter illustrate the mechanics of exploitation, they also highlight the necessity for robust security practices in software development.

Chapter 6: Malware Analysis using Assembly

Malware analysis is an essential skill in cybersecurity, allowing analysts to understand, detect, and mitigate threats posed by malicious software. Among various techniques employed for malware reverse engineering, static and dynamic analysis based on assembly language plays a critical role. This chapter delves into the intricacies of analyzing malware using assembly, equipping analysts with the knowledge necessary to dissect and understand malicious binaries.

Understanding Assembly Language

Assembly language is a low-level programming language that closely corresponds to a computer's machine code instructions. Because it operates at such a low level, assembly language provides a direct mapping to the underlying architecture of the CPU. This makes it the language of choice for those who need to interact closely with the hardware, such as in malware analysis.

The Basics of Malware

Malware encompasses various forms of malicious software, including viruses, worms, trojans, ransomware, and spyware. Each type behaves differently but typically seeks to perform unauthorized actions on the host system. Understanding the fundamentals of how malware functions is crucial before diving into assembly analysis.

Setting Up the Analysis Environment

Before starting the analysis, setting up a secure and controlled environment is imperative. Key components of a malware analysis workspace include:

Virtual Machines (VMs): Utilize VMs to isolate malware from the host environment, allowing for safe execution and observation.

Debuggers and Disassemblers: Tools such as OllyDbg, x64dbg, IDA Pro, and Ghidra are invaluable for stepping through code and translating machine instructions into human-readable assembly language.

Network Monitoring Tools: Tools like Wireshark can monitor outbound connections, which is useful for analyzing network-based malware behavior.

Static Analysis Tools: Additional tools such as PEiD and CFF Explorer can help identify the properties and structure of executable files.

Static Analysis: Decoding the Binary

Static analysis involves examining the malicious binary without executing it. The primary goal is to gather information about its structure and identify potentially harmful instructions. Here's how to carry out effective static analysis using assembly language.

1. File Format Examination

Every executable file begins with a header that contains metadata, such as the file format (EXE, ELF, etc.) and sections (text, data, import/export, etc.). Tools like PE Explorer can help examine these characteristics in Windows binaries.

2. Disassembly

Using disassembly tools, the binary code is translated into assembly language. The disassembler breaks down the binary into meaningful assembly instructions, allowing the analyst to comprehend what the code intends to do.

3. Control Flow Analysis

Understanding how the malicious code flows is crucial to discerning its behavior. Reviewing function calls, jump instructions (e.g., `jmp`, `je`, `jne`), and loops is essential to mapping out how the malware operates.

4. Identifying Strings

Malware often contains strings that reveal its purpose or command and control (C2) server. By scanning for ASCII or Unicode strings within the binary, analysts can uncover insights into the functionality of the malware.

Dynamic Analysis: Observing Behavior

Dynamic analysis allows analysts to see how malware behaves during execution. This involves running the malware in a controlled environment and observing its interactions with the system.

1. Setting Breakpoints

Using a debugger, set breakpoints at critical points in the execution path. This allows you to pause execution and inspect the state of the program, including registers and memory locations.

2. Monitoring API Calls

Malware frequently leverages system API calls to perform its functions, such as file manipulation or network connections. Tools like API Monitor can help trace these interactions.

3. Heap and Stack Analysis

Examining the stack and heap can provide additional insight into the state of the application during execution. Analyzing how the malware allocates memory can reveal hidden functionalities or data exfiltration methods.

Case Study: Analyzing a Simple Malware

To illustrate the concepts discussed, let's analyze a simple piece of malware using assembly language. Suppose we encounter a sample that exhibits the following behavior:

It opens a certain file on the system (e.g., a document).

It sends its data over a network socket to a remote server.
Step 1: Static Analysis

Upon loading the binary into a disassembler, we examine the PE header and locate the imports for

`CreateFile`, `Send`, and `CloseSocket`. String analysis reveals the IP address of the C2 server hardcoded into the binary.

Step 2: Dynamic Analysis

Next, we execute the malware in a controlled environment. Setting breakpoints on the aforementioned API calls allows us to monitor file access and data transmission activity. We observe that, upon execution, the malware opens a specified file and sends its contents to the identified remote server.

Malware analysis using assembly language is a powerful technique for uncovering the inner workings of malicious software. Through both static and dynamic analysis, security professionals can dissect malware to understand its objectives, mechanics, and potential impact on systems. As adversaries continue to evolve their strategies, the ability to analyze and reverse engineer malware remains a vital skill in the cybersecurity landscape.

How Malware Uses Assembly to Evade Detection

One of the more technical and effective tactics involves the use of assembly language—an intermediate layer between high-level programming languages and machine code. This chapter explores how malware utilizes assembly to create undetectable payloads, focusing on specific techniques, examples, and countermeasures.

Understanding Assembly Language

Assembly language is a low-level programming language that provides a symbolic representation of a computer's binary code. It closely reflects the architecture of the underlying hardware, allowing developers to write programs with fine-grained control over system resources and execution flow. For malware authors, this granular control is essential when crafting code that must run discretely, avoiding detection by security measures such as antivirus software, intrusion detection systems, or behavioral analysis tools.

Advantages of Using Assembly in Malware Development

Obfuscation: Assembly code is inherently complex and not easily read or understood by laypersons or automated code analysis tools. This complexity provides an effective layer of obfuscation.

Custom Functionality: Assembly allows malware authors to implement functionalities that may not be easily achievable in higher-level languages, such as real-time hook setting or direct manipulation of hardware.

Size Efficiency: Assembly code can be extremely compact, enabling malware to remain small and avoid raising alarms due to unusual file sizes.

Bypassing Security Checks: By manipulating the way instructions are executed at the processor level, malware can exploit vulnerabilities in security measures, including altering control flow to avoid detection.

Case Study: Injecting Malicious Code

To illustrate the power of assembly in evading detection, let's examine a simple example: injecting malware into a legitimate process. This technique is often referred to as "process injection," and it allows the attacker to run malicious code within the context of a trusted program, making it harder to detect.

Example: A Simple Assembly Injection

Below is a simplified example of how assembly can be used to inject code into another process. Although complete implementation would require more setup and context (such as payload creation and the target process), we'll focus on the assembly code aspect of the operation.

```assembly
section .text

global _start

_start:
```

; Open target process (for demonstration, we're not executing it) mov eax, 0x5 ; syscall number for sys_open

lea ebx, [filename] xor ecx, ecx   ; flags

int 0x80   ; call kernel

; Inject payload

mov ebx, eax   ; handle of the opened file mov edx, payload ; address of the payload mov ecx, [payload_size]

; Write the payload to the memory of process mov eax, 0x4   ; syscall number for sys_write int 0x80   ; call kernel

; Exit cleanly

mov eax, 0x1   ; syscall number for sys_exit xor ebx, ebx   ; return code 0

int 0x80   ; call kernel

section .data

filename   db   'target_process.exe',   0   payload   db 'malicious_code_here', 0 payload_size db 18 ; Size of the payload

```

### Explanation of the Code

**System Calls**: The assembly code utilizes system calls to perform operations such as opening a target process and writing the payload to memory. This low-level interaction makes it difficult for high-level detection tools to recognize unauthorized behavior.
```

Direct Memory Access: The ability to directly manipulate the process memory allows the payload to be injected into the execution flow of a high-trust process, escaping scrutiny from security mechanisms.

Obfuscation Techniques: The payload itself can be obfuscated further using various methods (e.g., encoding, control flow obfuscation) to make it even less recognizable to static code analysis.

Countermeasures

Detection Techniques

Understanding how malware utilizes assembly to evade detection equips security professionals with the knowledge needed to better protect systems. Here are some countermeasures to consider:

Behavioral Analysis: Implement systems that can detect abnormal behaviors in processes, such as unusual memory writes or execution flows.

Memory Scanning: Regularly scan memory for known patterns of injected code, especially within high-value processes.

Signature-based Detection: Develop advanced heuristics and signatures specifically for recognizing unusual assembly code patterns related to known malicious behaviors.

Sandboxing: Run processes in isolated environments to observe their behavior without risking critical system resources, allowing for detection of unusual activities.

Education and Awareness: Train staff on the latest

attack vectors and defensive coding practices to mitigate risks associated with malware development.

Malware authors exploit assembly language not only for its efficiency and low-level control but also for its natural capacity to obfuscate malicious intent. Understanding these tactics is crucial for cybersecurity professionals tasked with defending against increasingly sophisticated threats.

Dissecting Malware Code and Understanding Its Behavior

This chapter aims to provide a comprehensive understanding of malware analysis techniques, including static and dynamic analysis, along with practical examples to illustrate these concepts.

Understanding Malware

Before diving into dissection techniques, it's essential to understand what malware is. Malware, short for malicious software, encompasses a variety of software designed to harm, exploit, or otherwise compromise computer systems, networks, or devices. Typical forms of malware include viruses, worms, trojans, ransomware, spyware, and adware.

Each type of malware has its own unique characteristics and methods of operation. Therefore, recognizing these distinctions is crucial for effective analysis and response.

Static Analysis: A First Look at Malware

Static analysis involves examining the malware code without executing it. This method allows analysts to gather information about the program's structure, strings, functions, and overall behavior without the risk of infection. There are several tools and techniques to perform static analysis.

Tools for Static Analysis

Disassemblers and Decompilers: Tools like IDA Pro, Ghidra, and Radare2 allow analysts to convert binary files into assembly or high-level code, enabling a better understanding of what the malware does.

String Analysis: Tools such as `strings` (a Unix utility) can extract human-readable strings from binary files. Analyzing these strings can provide clues about the malware's capabilities, such as URLs, file paths, or embedded commands.

Hex Editors: Programs like HxD or Hex Fiend allow analysts to view and modify the raw bytes of a file. This can be especially useful for identifying embedded resources or checking for unusual file structures.

Example of Static Analysis

Imagine we have a suspicious executable file named `malware_sample.exe`. Using a disassembler, we can load the file and observe its functions.

After opening it in Ghidra, we identify a function that takes user input.

Analyzing associated strings reveals URLs that suggest communication with a Command and Control (C2) server.

Further investigation shows the presence of API calls that indicate potential file manipulation, such as

`CreateFile`, `WriteFile`, and `DeleteFile`.

From these findings, we can infer that this malware sample is likely designed to communicate with a malicious server, possibly to exfiltrate data.

Dynamic Analysis: Observing Malware Behavior

While static analysis is beneficial, dynamic analysis involves executing the malware in a controlled environment to observe its behavior in real-time. This method provides insights into how the malware interacts with the operating system and network, what file changes it makes, and how it propagates.

Setting Up a Safe Environment

Dynamic analysis is typically conducted in a sandbox environment to prevent malware from affecting production systems. Tools such as Cuckoo Sandbox, Any.Run, or VMware can be utilized to create isolated environments for safe execution.

Observing Malware Behavior

File System Changes: Analysts can monitor the creation, deletion, or modification of files. Tools like Process Monitor can aid in tracking these activities.

Network Traffic Analysis: Monitoring network traffic during execution is key to understanding how malware communicates with external servers. Tools like Wireshark can provide visibility into outgoing connections.

Process Behavior: Observing which processes are spawned by the malware can help identify its capabilities and intentions. Tools like Process Explorer can facilitate this analysis.

Example of Dynamic Analysis

Continuing with the `malware_sample.exe`, we execute it in a sandboxed environment.

We utilize Process Monitor to find that it creates a file in the user's AppData directory.

Wireshark reveals that the malware attempts to connect to the previously identified C2 URL.

Analyzing outgoing packets shows that the malware sends out a compressed archive of data pulled from local files.

These behaviors confirm our suspicions from the static analysis phase, indicating that the malware is designed for data theft.

Dissecting malware code and understanding its behavior is a critical skill for cybersecurity professionals. By employing both static and dynamic analysis techniques, analysts can uncover the intentions and functionalities of malicious software. This understanding not only aids in mitigating current threats but also contributes to developing more effective defense mechanisms against future attacks.

As malware continues to evolve in complexity, the importance of thorough analysis cannot be overstated. By mastering these techniques, security practitioners can stay one step ahead in the relentless battle between cyber defense and cyber offense.

Chapter 7: Remote Code Execution and Assembly

This chapter delves into the concepts of remote code execution, examining how such exploits occur, the implications they have for cybersecurity, and how knowledge of assembly language can bolster defense mechanisms.

7.1 Understanding Remote Code Execution

Remote Code Execution is a potent form of attack that allows an attacker to run arbitrary code on a remote machine without the owner's consent. This can lead to a variety of malicious outcomes, including data theft, data corruption, and the establishment of backdoors for further exploits. To effectively combat RCE, it is crucial to understand how such vulnerabilities originate.

7.1.1 Common Vulnerabilities Leading to RCE

RCE vulnerabilities often stem from a variety of coding errors and misconfigurations, including but not limited to:

Buffer Overflows: When a program writes more data to a buffer than it can hold, it may overwrite adjacent memory, allowing an attacker to inject malicious code.

Unsafe Deserialization: When programs deserialize data from untrusted sources, attackers can manipulate that data to execute arbitrary code.

Injection Flaws: This encompasses SQL injection, command injection, and other forms, where the attacker injects malicious commands into a program that executes them.

Understanding these vulnerabilities requires an in-depth grasp of how software is constructed and how various programming languages interact with hardware.

7.2 The Mechanics of Remote Code Execution

To illustrate how remote code execution works, we can consider a simplified model using a web application as an example. When a user sends a request to a web server, it processes this input, often relying on dynamic evaluations within code. If the input is not adequately sanitized, it opens the door for code injection attacks.

7.2.1 Attack Vectors

Web Applications: Attackers can exploit web applications (like those built on PHP or JavaScript) by injecting scripts or commands.

Network Services: Exposed server software running on various ports may be vulnerable, especially if outdated or improperly configured.

Misconfigured APIs: Poorly secured APIs can be exploited to execute arbitrary commands on the server.

7.3 Assembly Language and Lower-Level Programming

While modern programming languages abstract away the complexities of hardware interactions, understanding assembly language is vital for cybersecurity professionals. Assembly language is a low-level programming language that provides a symbolic representation of a computer's machine code.

7.3.1 The Role of Assembly in Cybersecurity

Vulnerability Analysis: Analyzing vulnerabilities often requires understanding the assembly code generated by compiling high-level languages. By examining the assembly, security analysts can identify buffer overflows and other weaknesses.

Exploit Development: Crafting effective exploits often necessitates manipulating system calls and memory addresses—skills that are honed through knowledge of assembly language.

Reverse Engineering: In the context of threat analysis, being proficient in assembly language allows for deeper insights into malware behavior, enabling defenders to develop more robust defenses.

7.4 Defensive Strategies Against RCE

Defending against remote code execution exploits requires a multi-layered approach: #### 7.4.1 Code Reviews and Static Analysis

Regular code reviews and the use of static analysis tools can help identify and remedy vulnerabilities before code is deployed. This process should involve both automated tools and manual inspection.

7.4.2 Input Validation and Sanitization

Implementing strict input validation techniques can significantly reduce the risk of RCE attacks. This involves ensuring that all inputs conform to expected formats and sanitizing inputs to neutralize potentially dangerous content.

7.4.3 Use of Security Mechanisms

Employing security mechanisms such as address-space

layout randomization (ASLR), data execution prevention (DEP), and control flow guard (CFG) can greatly increase the difficulty for attackers attempting to exploit RCE vulnerabilities.

7.5 The Future of Remote Code Execution

As technology continues to advance, RCE vulnerabilities will persist but evolve. With the rise of cloud computing, IoT devices, and increasingly complex software architectures, cybersecurity professionals must remain vigilant. Understanding the foundational aspects of programming and assembly language provides the necessary ammunition against potential threats.

By understanding how these exploits occur and leveraging knowledge of assembly language, cybersecurity professionals can better protect critical infrastructure and sensitive information.

RCE Exploits in Assembly

Understanding how these exploits work, particularly at the assembly level, is essential for cybersecurity professionals and enthusiasts. This chapter presents an overview of RCE exploits, focusing on assembly language concepts and providing script examples to demonstrate how these exploits can be implemented and mitigated.

Understanding RCE Exploits

What is Remote Code Execution?

Remote Code Execution is a vulnerability that allows an attacker to control a target machine or application remotely. Typically, this occurs when an application improperly handles input data, allowing the attacker to manipulate the execution flow of the program. RCE vulnerabilities can originate in various software components, including web applications, network services, and desktop applications.

Common Types of RCE Vulnerabilities

Buffer Overflows: This occurs when data exceeds the boundaries of allocated memory buffer, allowing attackers to overwrite the return address on the stack.

Command Injection: This happens when user inputs are not properly sanitized, allowing attackers to inject and execute commands on the host system.

File Inclusion Vulnerabilities: Attackers can exploit these vulnerabilities to include arbitrary files, leading to code execution.

Deserialization Issues: Improperly performed deserialization can allow malicious data to execute arbitrary code during the reconstitution of an object.

Assembly Language Basics

Assembly language serves as a low-level programming language that is closely tied to a computer's architecture. Understanding assembly is crucial when analyzing binary exploits, as it directly interacts with the system's hardware and memory. A basic assembly instruction set typically includes operations such as data movement, arithmetic operations, logical operations, and control flow management.

Key Assembly Instructions

MOV: Move data from one location to another.

CALL: Call a procedure or function.

RET: Return from a procedure or function.

JMP: Jump to a specified address.

CMP: Compare two values, often used in conditional branches.

INT: Trigger an interrupt, which can invoke system calls. ## Example: A Simple RCE Exploit Script

This section provides an illustrative example of a buffer overflow RCE exploit written in assembly, focusing on a hypothetical vulnerable application.

The Vulnerable Application

Consider a simple C program that reads user input into a stack-allocated buffer without proper bounds checking:

```c
#include <stdio.h> #include <string.h>

void vulnerable_function(char *user_input) { char buffer[64];

strcpy(buffer, user_input); // Vulnerable to buffer overflow
}

int main() {

char input[128]; printf("Enter some text:\n");

fgets(input,                sizeof(input),                stdin);
vulnerable_function(input); return 0;
}
```

```
```

Anatomy of the Exploit

Buffer Overflow: The `strcpy` function does not check the length of the input, allowing an attacker to overflow the buffer and overwrite the return address.

Payload Construction: The attacker crafts a payload containing shellcode and a new return address that points to their code.

Assembly Script for Exploit

Below is an assembly code that simulates the exploit process:

```assembly
assembly section .text global _start

_start:

; This is an example payload to execute. xor rax, rax    ; Clear the RAX register

mov rdi, rax   ; Set RDI (first argument) to 0 mov rsi, rax
        ; Set RSI (second argument) to 0 mov rdx, rax
        ; Set RDX (third argument) to 0 mov rax, 60
        ; SYS_exit

syscall; Invoke the syscall
```

How the RCE Works

Payload Execution: When the crafted payload is sent to the vulnerable application, the stack is compromised, and control is diverted to the attacker's shellcode.

Creating a Shell: The above assembly code terminates the process, but a more complex payload could invoke a shell, giving full remote control.

Mitigating RCE Exploits ### Preventive Measures

Input Validation: Always validate and sanitize user inputs to prevent buffer overflows and command injections.

Use Safe Functions: Avoid unsafe functions like `strcpy` and prefer safer alternatives like `strncpy`.

Stack Canaries: Implement stack protection techniques such as stack canaries that detect overflow attempts.

Address Space Layout Randomization (ASLR): Make it difficult for attackers to predict the location of code in memory.

Regular Security Audits: Continuously review and audit code for vulnerabilities.

By analyzing vulnerable code and constructing exploit scripts, professionals can develop a deeper comprehension of the nuances of RCE vulnerabilities. Moreover, emphasizing preventive measures is vital in safeguarding systems from potential attacks.

Writing and Executing Malicious Payloads

This chapter aims to provide a foundational understanding of writing simple malicious payloads in assembly and executing them in a controlled environment for educational purposes only. We will explore how such payloads can manipulate program execution flow and interact with system resources.

Disclaimer

This chapter is intended solely for educational and ethical purposes. Attempting to write or execute malicious software without explicit permission is illegal and unethical. Always ensure compliance with local laws and organizational policies when engaging in cybersecurity practices.

Understanding Assembly Language

Assembly language provides a direct way to manipulate hardware through machine instructions specific to a given architecture, often x86 or x86_64 for personal computers. It operates at a much lower level compared to high-level programming languages, giving developers fine-grained control over the system's processes.

The Structure of an Assembly Program

A basic assembly program consists of several components:

Data segment: Where variables are declared.

Text segment: Contains the executable instructions.

Code segment: Instructions that tell the CPU what tasks to execute. ### Example: Writing a Simple Payload

For educational purposes, we will write a simple assembly payload that demonstrates how to create a basic shellcode. This shellcode will spawn a shell (i.e., `/bin/sh` on Unix-like systems). We'll use NASM (Netwide Assembler) for assembling the code and an ELF (Executable and Linkable Format) binary for execution.

Step 1: Writing the Payload

Below is an example of a basic payload in x86 assembly that spawns a shell:

```assembly
section .text

global _start

_start:
; Push the string "/bin/sh"

xor rax, rax   ; Clear RAX register

push rax      ; NULL terminator for the string push
0x68732f2f         ; Push the string "//sh"

push 0x6e69622f    ; Push the string "/bin"

mov rdi, rsp  ; Set RDI to point to the string "/bin/sh"

; Prepare to call execve

xor rsi, rsi    ; argv = NULL xor rdx, rdx        ; envp = NULL

mov rax, 59          ; syscall: execve syscall    ; Invoke the syscall
```

The key instructions in this payload are:

Push: This is used to place the string `"/bin/sh"` onto the stack.

mov and syscall: These are critical for setting up and executing system calls, in this case, `execve` to spawn a shell.

Step 2: Assembling the Payload

To assemble and link the payload, save the above code to a file named `shellcode.asm` and use the following commands:

```bash
nasm -f elf64 -o shellcode.o shellcode.asm ld -o shellcode
shellcode.o
```

This will create an executable file named `shellcode`. ###
Executing the Payload

Once compiled, the malicious payload can be executed on
a compatible system. Before executing any payload,
ensure that you are in a safe environment, such as a
virtual machine or a controlled lab setup.

Run the following command in your terminal:

```bash
./shellcode
```

If executed successfully, this payload will spawn a shell
(`/bin/sh`), providing command-line access. ##
Analyzing the Payload

Understanding how this payload works is crucial. The
process entails:

Stack Manipulation: We pushed data onto the stack to
create our string.

System Calls: By invoking the `execve` system call, we
request the operating system to execute the program
located at our specified address in memory.

Ethical Considerations

It cannot be stressed enough that understanding and experimenting with malicious payloads should only be done in a safe and legal environment. Always ensure ethical boundaries are respected and avoid any unauthorized access to systems.

While this knowledge can enhance one's understanding of system vulnerabilities, it is imperative to use it responsibly within the framework of ethical hacking and cybersecurity practices. Continuous learning and experimentation in a controlled, ethical manner can help build a robust comprehension of both offensive and defensive security strategies.

Chapter 8: Address Space Layout Randomization (ASLR) and DEP Protection

This chapter delves into the mechanisms of ASLR and DEP, their implementation at the assembly language level, and their significance in bolstering application security.

8.1 Understanding ASLR

ASLR is a security technique that randomizes the memory addresses used by system and application processes. By shifting the locations of key data structures, ASLR makes it considerably harder for attackers to predict the locations of specific functions or buffers within an application.

8.1.1 How ASLR Works

ASLR operates by randomizing the following elements in memory:

The base address of the executable code.

The addresses of DLLs (Dynamic Link Libraries) loaded into the process.

The locations of stack, heap, and memory segments.

When a program is executed, ASLR modifies the memory layout, which means that even if the same program is run multiple times, it will have a different memory layout each time. This unpredictability significantly increases the difficulty of successful exploitation.

8.1.2 Implementing ASLR in Assembly

The implementation of ASLR requires no specific assembly code from the programmer's side; instead, it is enabled at the compiler or operating system level. However, understanding how memory allocation works at the assembly level can provide better insights into how ASLR impacts program execution.

For instance, when a process is loaded into memory, the operating system assigns random addresses for its various segments - text (code), data (static variables), heap (dynamic memory), and stack (local variables). A simplified view of how a function might be invoked in a randomized environment can be shown as follows in pseudocode:

```assembly
; Calculate the address of the function
mov eax, [base_address_of_module] ; Load the base address
add eax, offset_to_function      ; Add offset to get address of the function call eax    ; Call the function
```

In this case, the `base_address_of_module` would vary with each execution due to ASLR, thus ensuring that the `offset_to_function` will always lead to a different location.

8.2 Understanding DEP

Data Execution Prevention (DEP) is another crucial security mechanism that restricts the execution of code in certain regions of memory, specifically where executable code should not reside. It mitigates a range of memory-related attacks, including buffer overflows.

8.2.1 How DEP Works

DEP marks specific areas of memory as non-executable, meaning that the processor will not run any code placed in those regions. The fundamental memory areas typically protected include:

The stack: Used for local variables and function calls.

The heap: Used for dynamic memory allocation.

In most systems, DEP is enabled by default, providing an additional layer of protection even if ASLR is not enabled.

8.2.2 Implementing DEP in Assembly

The enforcement of DEP is largely handled by the operating system, and generally does not require specific code changes. However, an assembly programmer must understand how to structure their application to avoid putting executable code in non-executable regions.

For example:

```assembly
section .data
; Non-executable data section
my_data db 'Hello, World!', 0

section .text
global _start

_start:
call my_function

my_function:
; Function logic here
ret
```

Here, the `.data` section contains non-executable data,

while the `.text` section is marked executable. By adhering to this structure, the assembly application remains compliant with DEP protocols.

8.3 The Synergy Between ASLR and DEP

When ASLR and DEP are used together, they create a robust line of defense against memory-based vulnerabilities. ASLR randomizes memory addresses, making it hard for attackers to guess where to inject malicious code. Simultaneously, DEP prevents the execution of code in regions that should only contain data.

This combined approach drastically reduces the success rate of traditional buffer overflow attacks, as attackers no longer have straightforward means to exploit known memory addresses.

By understanding the interplay and implementation of ASLR and DEP, assembly programmers can write more secure applications, contributing to overall system resilience against cyber threats. As we move into the next chapter, we will continue exploring advanced security mechanisms that further enhance application security.

Overcoming ASLR Using Assembly

This chapter explores the principles of ASLR, the challenges it presents, and how assembly language can be employed to circumvent it in a controlled and educational manner.

Understanding ASLR

ASLR works by loading executable modules into random memory addresses each time a program is executed. For instance, the base address of the executable, dynamic libraries (such as DLLs in Windows or shared objects in Unix-like systems), the stack, and the heap are randomized. This makes it difficult for an attacker to predict these memory addresses, which is vital when attempting to exploit vulnerabilities such as buffer overflows or format string attacks.

ASLR is highly effective in complicating attacks, but it is not foolproof. Exploit development has continued to evolve, leading to techniques that can bypass these defenses. One such method involves the use of assembly language to manipulate the behavior of programs at a low level, allowing attackers—with the right knowledge— to gather the necessary information to defeat ASLR.

The Structure of ASLR

To appreciate how to overcome ASLR, let's delve deeper into how it is structured and implemented:

Randomization of the Address Space: ASLR shifts the locations of segments in memory. For every execution of a binary, the data associated with its runtime aspects, such as libraries and stack positions, are fundamentally altered.

Utilization of Position Independent Executables (PIE): Compilers can create position-independent code that enables executables to be loaded at random addresses, further enhancing ASLR. This functionality is often embedded in modern build tools and is a standard practice in secure coding.

Predictable Patterns: While ASLR can randomize segments, it does so based on specific algorithms dependent on entropy, which can sometimes be predicted. An attacker may leverage side-channel information or brute-force techniques to determine the layout.

Assembly Language: The Low-Level Powerhouse

Assembly language is a low-level programming language that provides direct manipulation of the hardware and memory. By using assembly, an attacker can write tailored exploits that directly interact with an application's memory space. Understanding assembly is critical for offensive security practitioners aiming to comprehend and analyze vulnerabilities effectively.

Bypassing ASLR

There are several methods by which ASLR can potentially be bypassed using assembly:

Information Leakage: Attackers can exploit bugs in a program to leak memory addresses. For example, if a program inadvertently exposes a pointer to a critical memory location, this can reveal where the code or critical data structures are located.

Brute-force Techniques: If the potential addresses are known to have limited values (for instance, when the entropy of ASLR is reduced), attackers may create a brute-force script to attempt various memory addresses until the correct one is found.

JIT-ROP (Just-In-Time Return Oriented Programming): Taking advantage of Just-In-Time compilation, an attacker can manipulate the program's flow to perform arbitrary code execution without needing to know the actual address of the gadget instructions.

Returns in the Wrong Context: By carefully

constructing return addresses in stack memory, an attacker can manipulate the control flow of an application to execute the shellcode.

A Practical Example in Assembly

Let's consider a hypothetical application vulnerable to buffer overflow where the stack is randomized, but some information leakage occurs due to a faulty logging function. The attacker could write a small assembly snippet that retrieves the stack pointer and manipulates the return address.

```assembly
segment.text global _start

_start:

; assume buffer is at esp + 0x10 and contains the return address mov eax, [esp + 0x10]  ; load the return address

add eax, offset my_function ; target function offset

mov [esp + 0x10], eax ; overwrite to execute desired function

; Execute the function call eax

my_function:

; Place the desired execution code here

; For example, spawn a shell or escalate privileges mov eax, 1 ; sys_exit

xor ebx, ebx ; return 0 int 0x80
```

In this example, the attacker assumes they can deduce the offset for `my_function` and can overwrite a return address in a buffer on the stack. Although it is a simplified

104

representation, it highlights how low-level assembly can directly manipulate execution flow, overriding ASLR protections.

Safeguarding Against Assembly Level Attacks

While the chapter focuses on overcoming ASLR, it is crucial to discuss countermeasures:

Enhanced Randomization: Increase the entropy of ASLR by implementing more unpredictable algorithms or structures.

Stack Canaries: Use stack canaries to detect buffer overflows and terminate the process before an exploitation can occur.

Memory Protection Techniques: Implement Non-Executable (NX) stack configurations and Data Execution Prevention (DEP) to prevent execution of unintended code paths.

Canary Checks for return-oriented programming (ROP); Implementing ROP-aware mechanisms can thwart attempts to leverage memory layout manipulations.

While ASLR represents a substantial advance in the fight against exploitative techniques in software, understanding its limitations and the potential of assembly programming allows both attackers and defenders to refine their approaches. The balance between exploiting vulnerabilities and implementing defensive programming is a dynamic battlefield in cybersecurity.

Techniques for Circumventing Data Execution Prevention (DEP)

DEP helps mitigate risks associated with buffer overflows and code injection attacks by marking areas of memory as non-executable, thereby preventing the execution of arbitrary code in those regions. However, adversaries continually seek ways to bypass this protection mechanism. This chapter delves into techniques for circumventing DEP using assembly language, emphasizing an understanding of these methods to enhance defensive strategies in cybersecurity.

Understanding DEP

Before exploring circumvention techniques, it's essential to understand how DEP functions. Typically, DEP operates in two modes:

Hardware-enforced DEP: Utilizes CPU features (like NX bit) to mark memory pages as non- executable or executable.

Software-enforced DEP: Relies on the operating system to enforce memory protections and apply mitigation strategies.

DEP can be applied to processes on the operating system level, preventing executable code from running in data segments like the heap and stack. As cybersecurity experts, the intention of studying DEP circumvention techniques is not to engage in malicious activities but to comprehend the adversarial strategies that exist.

Techniques for Circumventing DEP

1. Return-Oriented Programming (ROP)

Description

Return-Oriented Programming is a sophisticated exploitation technique that allows an attacker to execute code in the presence of DEP. Instead of injecting their malicious code into a process, ROP leverages small snippets of existing executable code, called "gadgets," which end in a return instruction. By carefully chaining these gadgets together, the attacker manipulates the call stack to achieve their objectives.

Implementation Steps

Gadget Identification: An attacker disassembles the target binary to identify useful gadget locations in executable memory sections.

ROP Chain Construction: A payload is constructed that includes the addresses of these gadgets in a specific order to achieve desired functionality.

Buffer Overflow Payload: The attacker crafts a buffer overflow exploit that overwrites the return address on the stack to point to the first gadget.

```assembly
; Example assembly snippet illustrating a simple ROP chain mov eax, [esp + 4*arg1] ; load first argument

call [address_of_first_gadget] ; call first gadget ret ; continue to chain
```

2. Function Pointer Overwriting

Description

Another method to bypass DEP is through manipulating

function pointers, particularly in languages like C or C++ where function pointers are frequently utilized. By overwriting a valid function pointer, an attacker can redirect execution flow to their malicious payload.

Implementation Steps

Identify Function Pointers: Locate function pointers in the target application (often found in vtables or callback functions).

Overwrite Pointer: Use a buffer overflow or a similar vulnerability to overwrite the function pointer with the address of the attacker's shellcode or ROP chain.

Trigger Pointer Execution: Cause the program to invoke the overwritten function pointer, executing the attacker's payload.

```assembly
; Overwriting a function pointer in assembly

mov [address_of_function_pointer], address_of_payload ; overwrite pointer call [address_of_function_pointer] ; invoke the payload
```

3. Code Injection through Non-Executable Regions
Description

While DEP restricts execution in certain memory regions, attackers can exploit other regions, particularly those marked writable. By injecting code into writable segments and utilizing techniques that could obfuscate or disguise the payload, attackers may bypass DEP protections.

Implementation Steps

Identify Writable Memory Regions: Examine the target application to find writable, executable memory segments.

Inject Code: Using techniques like heap spraying or just-in-time (JIT) compilation, inject the shellcode into these writable segments.

Execution Trigger: Execute the injected code by exploiting vulnerabilities that allow for execution.

```assembly
; Example of injecting code into writable memory mov eax, address_of_writable_memory

mov [eax], your_shellcode ; write shellcode into memory
jmp eax ; jump to the injected shellcode
```

4. Exploiting Memory Corruption Vulnerabilities
Description

Many applications suffer from memory corruption vulnerabilities that can be exploited to bypass DEP. These include use-after-free, double-free, or memory corruption due to buffer overflow. Understanding these vulnerabilities enables attackers to influence execution flow strategically.

Implementation Steps

Identify Vulnerability Points: Locate areas in the code that are susceptible to memory corruption.

Trigger Vulnerability: Craft inputs that exploit the memory corruption while manipulating control data (like metadata and pointers).

Redirection: Use the corrupted memory state to redirect execution to a legitimate code path that may lead to code execution.

```assembly
; Use-after-free technique illustrated

mov eax, [free_memory_pointer] ; load address of deallocated memory jmp eax ; jump to deallocated memory which may still hold valid code
```

Circumventing Data Execution Prevention is a complex endeavor that often requires a multifaceted approach. Understanding techniques such as ROP, function pointer manipulation, code injection, and exploiting memory corruption vulnerabilities illustrates the creativity of adversaries and the need for robust security defenses. As defenders in the cybersecurity realm, it is imperative to remain vigilant, continuously studying these methods to develop countermeasures and enhance the security posture of applications and systems.

Understanding these circumvention techniques aids in building resilient systems and fortifying defenses against malicious exploitation. Engaging in or promoting unethical activities is strictly condemned, and practitioners should always adhere to ethical guidelines in cybersecurity.

Chapter 9: Return-Oriented Programming (ROP) for Exploitation

ROP takes advantage of existing code sections in a program, often leveraging system libraries, to manipulate the flow of execution. This chapter delves into the underlying concepts of ROP, its mechanics, practical implementations, and countermeasures to mitigate its effectiveness.

9.1 Understanding ROP ### What is ROP?

Return-Oriented Programming is an exploitation technique that allows attackers to execute code by chaining together short sequences of legitimate instructions that end in a "return" instruction. These sequences, known as "gadgets," are typically small fragments of code that already exist in the memory of a running application or its libraries. By carefully selecting and sequencing these gadgets, attackers can construct a payload that effectively performs the desired actions without injecting any new executable code, thereby evading certain security mechanisms.

The Mechanics of ROP

At its core, ROP relies on the manipulation of the call stack. When a function in a program finishes executing, it typically returns control to the caller function using the return address stored on the stack. In ROP attacks, the attacker overwrites the return address to point to the first gadget they wish to execute.

Subsequent gadgets are lined up in such a way that they lead to the execution of a desired sequence of operations.

Components of ROP

Gadgets: Short instruction sequences ending with a `RET` (return) instruction. Gadgets are the building blocks of ROP payloads.

Chain: A sequence of gadgets that are chained together through the use of manipulated return addresses.

Stack Manipulation: The control of the call stack is crucial. Attackers often use buffer overflows or other vulnerabilities to change the return addresses.

Example of a ROP Chain

To illustrate how ROP chains operate, consider the following simplified example:

An attacker starts with a buffer overflow that allows them to control the return address of a function.

They identify the following gadgets in the binary:

`Gadget 1:` Load value into register A

`Gadget 2:` Perform an arithmetic operation

`Gadget 3:` Call system command

The return address of the overflowed buffer is overwritten with the address of `Gadget 1`. As `Gadget 1` executes, it moves to `Gadget 2` after completing its instructions. This process continues, executing `Gadget 3`, and ultimately achieving a task such as spawning a shell.

9.2 Finding Gadgets

Finding gadgets within a binary is a crucial part of preparing a ROP attack. Various tools and techniques can assist in this process:

Tools for ROP Gadget Discovery

ROPgadget: A popular tool that scans binaries to find ROP gadgets.

Radare2: An open-source reverse engineering framework that includes capabilities for gadget discovery.

Ropper: A tool that can identify ROP gadgets and provide them in a usable format, making the attack easier to orchestrate.

Manual Gadget Finding

For advanced practitioners, manually analyzing disassembled code can reveal gadgets. Understanding assembly language, control flow, and how functions interact with the stack is essential for this process.

9.3 Applications of ROP in Exploitation

ROP can be applied in various contexts, especially in scenarios where standard code injection methods are thwarted by security measures like Data Execution Prevention (DEP) or the use of non-executable memory.

Bypassing Protections

Data Execution Prevention (DEP): ROP circumvents DEP since it utilizes existing executable code rather than injecting new code.

Address Space Layout Randomization (ASLR): While ASLR randomizes memory addresses, ROP attacks may still be possible if the attacker can leak memory addresses or if the same libraries are loaded in predictable locations.

Stack Canary: Although stack canaries are designed to

detect buffer overflows, attackers can still leverage ROP if they can find a way to overwrite the return address without triggering the canary check.

9.4 Real-World Examples

Several notable vulnerabilities have employed ROP techniques to demonstrate their effectiveness:

The "JIT-ROP" Attack: This sophisticated technique leverages Just-In-Time (JIT) compilation in JavaScript engines, allowing attackers to chain gadgets in dynamically generated memory.

Exploits on Browsers: Many exploitation frameworks leverage ROP for browser vulnerabilities, especially focusing on bypassing mitigations present in modern browsers.

9.5 Countermeasures against ROP

As with any exploitation technique, robust defenses are crucial to mitigating ROP attacks. Common countermeasures include:

Control Flow Integrity (CFI): Implementing CFI helps ensure that control flow in programs adheres to valid paths, making it significantly harder for an attacker to predict and manipulate execution.

Stack Canaries: Safeguarding against stack buffer overflows can prevent attackers from overwriting return addresses.

Address Space Layout Randomization (ASLR):

Randomizing memory addresses for executables, libraries, and heap allocations can make it challenging to locate gadgets consistently.

Code Integrity Checks: Regularly verifying the integrity of code and checking for unexpected modifications can help detect tampering.

Return-Oriented Programming represents an ingenious adaptation of existing code for exploitation, cleverly bypassing security measures designed to prevent traditional attacks. Its versatility and effectiveness underline the importance of developing advanced defensive mechanisms to protect systems from such sophisticated threats.

Introduction to ROP and Its Importance in Exploits

One of the most sophisticated techniques to emerge in this arena is Return-Oriented Programming (ROP). At its core, ROP is a powerful method that circumvents traditional protections such as Execute Disable (XD) and Address Space Layout Randomization (ASLR). This chapter serves as an introduction to ROP, its fundamental principles, and its critical role in modern exploits, particularly when examined through the lens of assembly language.

The Basics of ROP

Return-Oriented Programming is a form of code reuse attack that allows an attacker to execute arbitrary code in the presence of security defenses that prevent the execution of injected code. Rather than introducing new code into a vulnerable application, ROP strings together existing snippets of executable code, known as "gadgets," that end in a return instruction. This characteristic is what differentiates ROP from traditional buffer overflow attacks.

What Is a Gadget?

A gadget is typically a small sequence of machine instructions ending with a return instruction. These gadgets are usually compiled into the program's memory space, existing within existing library modules or the application's binary itself. For instance, an attacker may leverage standard library functions or common application behaviors to craft a series of these gadgets that perform their intended malicious operations.

The success of ROP hinges on the availability of these gadgets within the application's memory. Thus, understanding how to identify and chain together these small fragments of executable code is essential for implementing an effective ROP exploit.

The Mechanics of ROP

The mechanics of ROP are best illustrated through a simplified example. Imagine an application vulnerable to a buffer overflow. When an attacker exploits this vulnerability, they can manipulate the stack and control the return addresses used during function calls. By overwriting these return addresses with the addresses of chosen gadgets, the attacker directs the program's control flow to execute a carefully crafted sequence of instructions.

Let's consider an assembly-level sequence:

Find Gadgets: The attacker identifies a series of

gadgets:

Gadget A: `mov eax, 0x1; ret`

Gadget B: `add ebx, eax; ret`

Gadget C: `mov ecx, ebx; ret`

Gadget D: `int 0x80; ret` (to call a system function)

Craft Payload: The attacker then constructs a payload that includes:

The buffer overflow data,

Overwritten return addresses pointing to Gadget A, Gadget B, Gadget C, and finally Gadget D.

Execution: When the exploit is executed, control transfers to Gadget A, which subsequently leads to Gadget B, and so forth until the intended malicious action is performed.

Importance of ROP in Exploits

ROP represents a significant advancement over previous exploitation techniques, largely due to its inherent stealthiness and adaptability to modern software protections. The importance of ROP in exploits can be summarized in several key aspects:

1. Bypassing Security Mechanisms

Many contemporary applications employ security mechanisms designed to thwart direct code injection attacks. ROP exploits leverage code already present in memory, making it challenging for static analysis and runtime protections to detect malicious intent. Therefore, ROP has gained prominence as a go-to technique in the attacker's toolkit.

2. Flexibility and Adaptability

ROP can be tailored to work against a wide range of software applications and environments. Attackers can dynamically adapt their exploits to utilize different gadgets depending on the specific configuration of the target, including different operating systems, architectures, and even the state of executable memory regions.

3. Collaborative Exploitation

ROP can be combined with other exploit strategies to enhance their effectiveness. For instance, attackers may use ROP in conjunction with other techniques, such as heap exploitation or integer overflows, to further widen their attack surface and increase the likelihood of success.

4. Evolution of Malware

The rise of ROP exploits illustrates a broader trend in malware development, where attackers continuously adapt to counter the latest defensive technologies. Understanding ROP provides security professionals with invaluable insight into the current threat landscape, enabling them to develop more robust defenses against these increasingly sophisticated attack vectors.

Return-Oriented Programming is a groundbreaking technique that has reshaped the landscape of software exploitation. By understanding the principles and mechanisms of ROP, security researchers and professionals can better prepare themselves to defend against sophisticated attacks.

Building and Exploiting ROP Chains in Assembly

This chapter will provide a comprehensive overview of ROP, including how to build ROP chains, the role of assembly language in ROP, and practical examples that illustrate these concepts in action.

Understanding the Basics of Control Flow and Stack Management

To grasp ROP, we must first understand its foundation — the stack and control flow of programs. When a function is called in a program, the address of the return instruction (the point where the function was called) is pushed onto the stack. When the function execution completes, the program counter (PC) jumps back to this address, allowing for seamless execution continuation. By manipulating the stack, an attacker can redirect the flow of execution to code segments that execute desirable (malicious) actions.

What is a ROP Chain?

A ROP chain consists of a sequence of gadget addresses that the attacker constructs to manipulate program flow. Gadgets are short sequences of machine code that end in a return instruction and can be found in the executable memory of a program or its linked libraries. By chaining these gadgets together, an attacker can perform a series of operations without injecting executable code — a technique particularly valuable in the context of modern exploit mitigations like DEP (Data Execution Prevention).

Building ROP Chains #### 1. Finding Gadgets

The first step in building a ROP chain is to identify available gadgets within your target executable and its libraries. This can be accomplished using tools such as ROPgadget, radare2, or ROPc. A gadget typically consists of a few assembly instructions, often assembled into a precise structure:

```assembly
pop rdi
ret
```

This simple gadget would pop the top value from the stack into the RDI register before returning to the next address on the stack.

2. Constructing the ROP Chain

Once you identify the available gadgets, you can begin constructing your ROP chain. This involves organizing the addresses of the gadgets in a specific sequence to achieve your exploit objectives. Consider the following general steps for ROP chain construction:

Identify the target function: Determine the final goal of your exploit - whether it's to execute a shell or call a specific function.

Prepare your stack: Using a combination of gadgets, structure the stack in a way that leads to the target function when the execution path is redirected.

Chain the gadgets: Ensure that the gadgets are chained in a sequence that allows the program flow to continue flowing through them correctly.

An example ROP chain could look like this:

```plaintext
[Address of gadget 1] // Pop argument for the next function [Address of gadget 2] // Call function using prepared arguments [Address of gadget 3] // Final return or jump to desired execution
```

3. Example of a ROP Chain

Let's assume that our goal is to call a function `win()` that takes no parameters. The ROP chain might look like this:

```plaintext
0x00401234: pop rdi ; ret

0x00000001; some address we'll pass to the next function
0x00401256: call win
```

In this scenario, gadget `0x00401234` will prepare the RDI register with `0x00000001`. Next, the call to

`win()` is executed via the subsequent gadget address.
Exploiting ROP Chains

Once the ROP chain is constructed, the next phase is execution—triggering the ROP chain through a vulnerability.

1. Triggering the Vulnerability

A buffer overflow vulnerability is often an ideal candidate for this exercise. By overflowing a buffer, an attacker can overwrite the return address on the stack to point to the beginning of the ROP chain.

```c
```

```
char buffer[128];

strcpy(buffer, user_input);  // User input can overflow
this buffer
```
```

#### 2. Delivering the ROP Payload

With the correct buffer overflow in place, the ROP payload
can be delivered, causing the processor to begin executing
the gadgets in your chain.

### Countermeasures Against ROP

While ROP chains are ingenious, many systems deploy
mitigations to counteract them. Techniques include:

**Address Space Layout Randomization (ASLR):**
Randomizes the memory addresses assigned to process
space, making it harder to accurately predict gadget
addresses.

**Control Flow Integrity (CFI):** Ensures that the
program executes only legitimate code according to its
control-flow graph.

**Stack Canaries:** Placing a known value on the stack
that changes if a buffer overflow occurs, thus signaling
potential overflow attempts.

By mastering the art of ROP, offensive security
professionals can elucidate deeper insights into system
architecture and security flaws, providing the necessary
knowledge to fortify systems against such attacks.
Understanding both the mechanics of assembly and the
```

landscape of vulnerability exploitation is essential for anyone aiming to excel in the field of cybersecurity.

Chapter 10: Techniques for Evasion: Avoiding Detection

Understanding these techniques is crucial not only for malicious actors but also for defenders who seek to protect their systems from these threats. By analyzing how attackers circumvent security measures, cybersecurity professionals can improve their detection and prevention capabilities.

1. Understanding Detection Mechanisms

Before delving into evasion techniques, it's essential to acknowledge how detection mechanisms operate. Security software typically relies on predefined signatures, heuristic analysis, and behavioral monitoring to identify malicious activity.

Signature-Based Detection: This involves matching the characteristics of a known threat against a database of signatures. Attackers often modify their payloads to avoid signature detection.

Heuristic Analysis: This approach uses algorithms to detect potentially malicious behavior by analyzing code for unusual patterns or functions. Concealing behaviors that trigger heuristics can help evade this method.

Behavioral Monitoring: Here, security systems observe activities and flag anomalies. By mimicking legitimate user behavior or using timing obfuscation, attackers can minimize their chances of being detected.

2. Code Obfuscation Techniques

Code obfuscation is a critical strategy for evasion. It involves altering the assembly code in ways that preserve functionality but obscure its intent.

2.1 Symbol Renaming

Attackers can change variable names and function identifiers to random strings. This makes static analysis more challenging, as the meaningful context is removed. For instance, renaming a function from

`maliciousFunction` to `a1b2C3`. ### 2.2 Control Flow Obfuscation

By altering the control flow of an assembly program, attackers can make it difficult for analyzers to follow execution paths. This can be accomplished by adding unnecessary jumps or conditional branches that don't serve a real purpose.

Example:

```assembly
mov eax, 1 jmp skip nop

nop skip:

mov ebx, 2
```

Even though `nop` instructions do nothing, they disrupt the flow and may confuse basic static analyzers. ### 2.3 Instruction Reordering

Rearranging the order of instructions without altering their semantic meaning can help evade detection mechanisms that assume a specific instruction sequence.

Example:

```assembly mov eax, 5
add eax, 2
```

Could be reordered as:

```assembly add eax, 2
mov eax, 5
```

While the end result remains unchanged, the new order may throw off pattern recognition algorithms. ## 3. Anti-Debugging Techniques

Modern security tools leverage debugging techniques to analyze suspicions processes. Attackers employ anti-debugging strategies to thwart such analyses.

3.1 Using Platform-Specific APIs

On Windows, for instance, functions like `IsDebuggerPresent` can check for a debugger. If a debugger is detected, the malicious code can alter its execution flow or exit entirely.

Example:

```assembly
call IsDebuggerPresent test eax, eax
jz not_debugged
```

3.2 Timing Attacks

By manipulating execution timing, attackers can detect whether their code is being run in a debug environment.

For example, introducing sleeps or busy loops that alter the timing of execution can reveal whether the code is being debugged based on how quickly it runs.

4. Polymorphism and Metamorphism

Polymorphic and metamorphic techniques aim to change the appearance of malicious code each time it is executed or propagated, making it harder for signature-based detection systems to identify it.

4.1 Polymorphism

This involves changing the variable names, encoding strings, and altering non-essential parts of the code while retaining the core logic.

4.2 Metamorphism

With metamorphic malware, the code can entirely restructure itself during execution. It can rewrite its own code in memory to present a different form each time it runs.

5. Leveraging Encryption and Packing

Encryption and packing serve as additional layers of protection against detection. ### 5.1 Code Packing

Packing tools compress and encrypt the original binary, making it unreadable to static analysis tools until it is unpacked upon execution.

5.2 Runtime Decryption

In this method, the malware decrypts itself in memory. This approach minimizes the chance of detection since the static analysis tools can only see the packed form.

Understanding evasion techniques in assembly goes

beyond mere curiosity; it is a fundamental skill for both attackers and defenders within cybersecurity. While attackers continuously develop new methods to avoid detection, defenders must adapt and enhance their detection capabilities.

Hiding Malicious Code and Evasion Tactics

This chapter delves into various techniques utilized in assembly to conceal malicious code and navigate around security protocols.

The Importance of Assembly Language in Cyber Threats

Assembly language serves as an intermediary between high-level programming languages and machine code. Its ability to provide granular control over the system's hardware makes it an attractive choice for cybercriminals. In cybersecurity, the two primary goals of malicious code are stealth and execution.

Assembly language assists attackers in achieving these goals due to its low-level nature, allowing them to manipulate the system directly without drawing attention.

Stealth Mechanisms

Code Obfuscation: Code obfuscation refers to the practice of modifying code in a way that makes it difficult to understand while maintaining its functionality. In assembly, techniques such as variable renaming and control flow transformations can be utilized.

Example: Altering the structure of a typical loop to

jump to different sections of code can confuse static analysis tools and make reverse engineering more challenging.

Packing: Packing involves compressing and encrypting the malware code to reduce its size and evade detection by antivirus programs. The packed code is unpacked at runtime, which can bypass many static detection systems.

Example: Tools such as UPX (Ultimate Packer for eXecutables) can be employed to pack executable files containing assembly code, making them look benign until executed.

Anti-Debugging Techniques: Attackers implement anti-debugging tactics to prevent security analysts from examining the behavior of malicious code.

Example: Using specific assembly instructions that trigger exceptions when a debugger is attached or checking the presence of debugging tools in the system environment can effectively thwart analysis.

Evasion Tactics

Code Injection: This strategy involves inserting malicious assembly code into a legitimate application. By doing so, the malware runs with the permissions of the affected software, making detection harder.

Example: An attacker can use techniques like function hooking or API hooking to redirect legitimate calls to malicious functionality embedded within a program.

Polymorphism: Polymorphic malware alters its code with each iteration while keeping the underlying functionality intact. This characteristic helps evade signature-based detection systems.

Example: An assembler program can employ techniques to modify opcode sequences or even shift instruction sequences around to create a different "look" without changing the program's behavior.

Rootkits and Kernel-Level Operations: By embedding the malicious code into the kernel or exploiting rootkits, attackers can achieve persistent and stealthy access to the system.

Example: Writing assembly routines that directly interact with kernel APIs to hide files and processes from detection by the operating system can significantly increase the longevity of the malicious presence.

Defense Mechanisms Against Malicious Code

While the strategies employed by attackers are formidable, cybersecurity professionals can employ several defenses to mitigate these threats.

Behavioral Analysis

Advanced security solutions are increasingly using behavioral analysis to identify anomalies in system behavior instead of relying solely on signature-based detection. By analyzing the behavior of programs in real-time, security systems can flag unusual actions that deviate from expected patterns.

Static and Dynamic Analysis

Static analysis examines the code structure without executing it, while dynamic analysis involves running the code in a controlled environment. Both approaches can help identify hidden malicious code.

Sandboxing and Honeypots

Running potentially harmful code in a sandbox or honeypot environment can allow analysts to observe its behavior without risking the primary environment. These techniques can provide insights into how malicious code operates and its evasion tactics.

The realm of cybersecurity constantly adapts to threats, as attackers leverage assembly language's capabilities to craft sophisticated and stealthy malicious code. Understanding the nuances of how malicious code can be hidden and the strategies used for evasion is essential for developing robust defenses.

Anti-Analysis Techniques in Assembly

One effective way they achieve this is through anti-analysis techniques. This chapter delves into these methods within the context of Assembly language, providing script examples that illustrate how malware can obfuscate its behavior, manipulate its execution environment, and hinder analysis efforts.

Understanding Anti-Analysis Techniques

Anti-analysis techniques are tactics employed by malware to avoid detection and analysis. These techniques can include:

Environment Checks: Malware can check for the presence of debugging tools, virtual machines, or sandbox environments; if detected, the code may alter its behavior or terminate execution.

Code Obfuscation: By obfuscating code, malware can make it difficult for analysts to understand its functionality.

Timing Checks: Malware can use timing-based checks to detect the speed of its execution environment, which can indicate whether it is running in a sandbox.

API Manipulation: Certain API calls will behave differently in a controlled environment, so malware can use these discrepancies to determine if it is being analyzed.

This chapter will explore these techniques with practical assembly script examples. ## Example 1: Environment Checks

One common method of detection is checking for particular processes or files that indicate the presence of a debugger or virtual environment. Below is an example script written in Assembly that demonstrates this technique.

Assembly Script Example: Environment Check

```assembly
```assembly section .text global _start

_start:

; Check for a debugger

xor eax, eax   ; Clear EAX

mov eax, 0x30      ; System call number for NtQueryInformationProcess

; Using a valid 'processId' to represent our current process
mov ebx, [processId]

mov ecx, 0x0 ; ProcessBasicInformation
```
```

```
mov edx, esp        ; Pointer to a buffer to retrieve info int
0x2E   ; Call the system service
```

```
; Evaluate if debugger is present (using some return value
checks) cmp dword [esp], 0
```

```
je not_debugger
```

```
; If debugger is detected, exit gracefully mov ebx, 0      ;
Exit code 0
```

```
mov eax, 1    ; System call number for exit
```

```
int 0x80      ; Exit program
```

```
not_debugger:
```

```
; Proceed with the main functionality
```

```
; Main code goes here
```
```
```

In this example, the assembly code attempts to query the process information to check if a debugger is present. Depending on the status returned, it may terminate execution or carry on with its intended functionality.

Example 2: Code Obfuscation

Obfuscating the code makes it difficult for analysts to discern what the malware is doing. Below is a simple example demonstrating this idea:

Assembly Script Example: Code Obfuscation

```
```assembly section .text global _start
```

```
_start:
```

```
; Original simple operation: x = a + b
```

133
```

```
; a = 5, b = 3
mov eax, 5
mov ebx, 3 add eax, ebx


; Obfuscated way of adding:
mov ecx, 5 xor edx, edx
inc edx        ; edx = 1
add ecx, edx  ; Now equivocal to adding 5 + 1 inc edx   ;
edx = 2
add ecx, edx  ; Now equivocal to adding 5 + 2
; This indirect operation gives the same result as intended
calculation.


; Proceed with using the result
; The rest of the malware code continues here...
```

In this obfuscation example, a straightforward addition operation is made unnecessarily complex. This obscured logic can confuse analysts trying to understand the code.

Example 3: Timing Checks

Malware can employ timing checks to differentiate between a real user environment and a sandbox or debugger. Here is a simple timing check:

Assembly Script Example: Timing Check

```assembly
```assembly section .text
```
```

```
global _start
_start:
; Get the current time
rdtsc   ; Read time-stamp counter into EDX:EAX
mov esi, eax   ; Store the lower 32-bits for later comparison
; Simulate some operation call some_function
; Check the time again
rdtsc   ; Read time-stamp counter again sub eax, esi
        ; Calculate elapsed time


; If time elapsed is too short, assume analysis cmp eax,
1000   ; Check if under 1ms
jl exit_analysis      ; Exit if under threshold
; Proceed with malicious behavior
; Main code goes here...
exit_analysis:
; Exit gracefully if under timing threshold mov eax, 1   ;
System call for exit xor ebx, ebx   ; Exit code 0
int 0x80
```
` ` `

This script utilizes the `RDTSC` instruction to measure how much time elapsed during execution. If the elapsed time falls below a specific threshold, it is likely that the execution environment is not genuine, prompting the malware to exit.

The examples provided illustrate how simple assembly code can incorporate checks and obfuscations that hinder analysis efforts. As threats evolve, so too must our defensive strategies, necessitating ongoing education and adaptation within the field. By recognizing these tactics, analysts can better prepare to deconstruct and mitigate the threats posed by sophisticated malware.

Conclusion

As we reach the end of our journey through the intricate world of assembly programming and its vital role in cyber security, it is clear that a strong understanding of low-level code is not just an asset but a necessity for anyone pursuing a career in this dynamic field. Throughout this book, we have explored how mastering assembly language enables you to uncover the inner workings of systems, identify vulnerabilities, and develop sophisticated defensive strategies against cyber threats.

We began by delving into the fundamentals of assembly programming, grasping its unique syntax and operations alongside the architecture of various processors. As we progressed, we examined how these concepts translate into practical applications in both offensive and defensive cyber security. You've learned not only how to write assembly code but also how to analyze and exploit it, providing a complete picture of what it means to operate at the low level.

Moreover, we have highlighted the importance of ethical considerations in your journey. The skills and knowledge you've gained should always be tempered with responsibility. Understanding the potential for harm should guide your actions as you navigate the thin line between offense and defense. The ability to break down systems can be a powerful tool against malicious actors, but it also requires a commitment to integrity and ethical practice.

As you move forward, we encourage you to cultivate your skills continually. The landscape of cyber security is ever-evolving, with new threats emerging daily. Embrace lifelong learning, seek out new challenges, and stay curious. Whether you decide to specialize in security research, penetration testing, or system defense, assembly programming will always be a crucial element of your toolkit.

Finally, remember that the knowledge you've gained in this book is just the beginning. The community of cyber security professionals is vast, and collaboration and sharing insights will only strengthen our defenses against the ever-growing tide of cyber threats. Engage with peers, contribute to projects, and share your discoveries with the world.

By unleashing the power of low-level code, you not only enhance your own capabilities but also contribute to building a more secure digital environment for all. The future of cyber security is in your hands—embrace it, innovate, and lead the charge against cyber threats.

Thank you for joining me on this journey through assembly programming and cyber security. I wish you the best of luck as you apply your newfound skills and knowledge in the ever-exciting world of technology and security.

Biography

Louis Madson is a passionate innovator and expert in the world of **Madson**, dedicated to sharing knowledge and empowering others through his writing. With a deep understanding of the subject and years of hands-on experience, Louis has become a trusted voice, guiding readers toward mastery with clarity and precision.

Beyond his expertise in **Madson**, Louis is an avid enthusiast of **Assembly programming language**, drawn to its raw power and intricate logic. His fascination with low-level computing fuels his relentless pursuit of knowledge, always pushing the boundaries of what's possible.

When he's not immersed in his craft, Louis enjoys exploring new technologies, solving complex coding puzzles, and inspiring others to embrace the art of problem-solving. His writing is more than just information—it's a **journey of discovery**, designed to ignite curiosity and empower readers to take action.

Through his eBook, Louis Madson invites you to dive deep into **Madson**, equipping you with the tools, insights, and inspiration to turn knowledge into expertise.

Glossary: Assembly Programming for Cyber Security

A

Address

The location in memory where data or instructions are stored. Each address corresponds to a specific byte in the computer's memory.

Assembler

A tool that translates assembly language code into machine code or object code. Assemblers convert human-readable instructions into a format that the CPU can execute.

Assembly Language

A low-level programming language that uses mnemonic codes and symbols to represent machine-level instructions. It provides a symbolic representation of a computer's instruction set architecture (ISA).

B

Buffer Overflow

A vulnerability that occurs when data written to a buffer exceeds its allocated size, potentially overwriting adjacent memory. This can lead to code execution or program crashes.

Byte

A unit of digital information consisting of eight bits. It is the basic addressable element in many computer architectures.

C

Calling Convention

A set of rules defining how functions receive parameters from a caller and how they return values. It includes the order of argument passing and stack management.

Code Injection

A technique where an attacker exploits a vulnerability to introduce malicious code into a program's execution context, often leading to unauthorized operations.

D

Debugging

The process of identifying and fixing bugs or vulnerabilities in a program. Debugging tools can provide insight into how the code executes at the assembly level.

Disassembler

A tool that converts machine code back into human-readable assembly code, making it easier for analysts to understand how software operates.

E

EIP (Extended Instruction Pointer)

A register in x86 architecture that holds the address of the next instruction to be executed. It plays a crucial role in instruction flow control.

Exploit

A piece of code or a technique that takes advantage of a vulnerability or flaw in software to perform unintended actions, such as executing arbitrary code.

F

Function Pointer

A variable that stores the address of a function, allowing dynamic execution of code. Function pointers are often used in exploit techniques.

Firmware

A type of software that provides low-level control for a device's specific hardware. Understanding firmware vulnerabilities is essential for cyber security practitioners.

G

GDB (GNU Debugger)

An open-source debugger that allows programmers to see what is happening inside a program while it executes or what it was doing at the moment it crashed. It supports assembly code debugging.

H

Hexadecimal

A base-16 number system that uses the digits 0-9 and the letters A-F. It is often used in assembly programming to represent binary data in a more human-readable form.

I

Instruction Set Architecture (ISA)

The part of the computer architecture related to programming. It includes the set of instructions that the CPU can execute.

NOP (No Operation)

An assembly instruction that does nothing and is often used for timing purposes or to create space in assembly code without altering machine execution flow.

M

Machine Code

The set of binary instructions that a CPU can directly execute. Machine code is generated from high-level code or assembly language through a compiler or assembler.

Malware

Malicious software designed to infiltrate, damage, or disable computers or networks. Understanding assembly is critical for analyzing and reversing malware.

P

Payload

The part of an exploit that performs the intended action, such as executing a command or installing malware.

Return Address

The address in the call stack where execution will continue after a function call. It is a key element in stack- based exploits like buffer overflows.

R

Reverse Engineering

The process of analyzing software to understand its structure, function, and behavior, often used to identify vulnerabilities or analyze malware.

ROP (Return-Oriented Programming)

An exploitation technique that involves chaining together

small sequences of existing code (gadgets) to perform arbitrary actions, bypassing certain security mechanisms.

S

Stack

A region of memory used for storing temporary data, such as function parameters, return addresses, and local variables. Stack overflows are common security vulnerabilities.

Shellcode

A small piece of code used as the payload in the exploitation process, often used to create a command shell or perform certain actions on a target system.

T

Trap

An exception condition that can interrupt the normal flow of execution, often used to handle errors or system calls in the operating system.

U

Utilization

In the context of assembly programming and performance, it refers to the efficiency with which CPU resources are used, such as instructions executed per clock cycle.

V

Vulnerability

A weakness in a system or application that can be exploited to gain unauthorized access or perform unauthorized actions.

Virtual Memory

A memory management capability that creates the illusion of a large address space, allowing systems to run larger applications than physically available memory.

W

Watchpoint

A debugging feature that automatically stops execution when the value of a variable changes, enabling detailed monitoring of program behavior.

XOR (Exclusive OR)

A bitwise logical operator used in many encryption and obfuscation techniques. It is often employed in assembly to combine or manipulate data efficiently.